ROUGHNECK PRETTYBOY

(Ideas on a Revolution)

By
Jay Lefebvre

Copyright © 2017 Jay Lefebvre
All rights reserved.
ISBN:0692843078
ISBN-13:978-0692843079

This book is for Mya. In all of her shades.

And for my family.

"We've made a war against drugs in a social and economic vacuum, until hopelessness and rage have the damned of our cities fighting for nothing more or less than human desire and profit, against which no one has ever developed a single viable weapons system."

-The Corner

PART ONE

1..

They sit in the middle of the fast food restaurant. They sit and talk quietly, laughing with their food, playfully and untroubled, they interact like loving people. The conversation between them goes slowly, they are in no hurry. They touch and seem to have a future. She looks like she is in her early thirties, and he the same. They don't notice me. The rebel in the movie? That one who squints his eyes and smiles and has had enough? That is me, without the pay or adoration.

I have nothing left, just guts and arrogance. I have lost my teeth and cut my arms, chased away dreams and written dark poetry. I have slept in my own urine and yelled for a revolution. I have done things the ordinary man would find hilarious.

I want to go to them, this crazy couple, and sit down. I want to look at them and tell them thank you. Tell them that tomorrow morning I am going to rehab and that they will be the last people I will be remembering. But I don't.

It is nice to see people like this, for too long I have been looking the other way. Angry at other happiness. I sit and eat and look out the window at people being people, sick and distressed, muzzled with the thoughts of too much to do. They rush from here to there, stepping off of curbs into their cars ready for whatever. They have no idea what we are capable of. They busy and keep their heads down, not intentionally, not from mania, but because it is. They have no idea that last week I threatened suicide. I called my family and told them I didn't want to be here any longer. These people, here, dressed in buttons and technology lighting their lives, outside on the pretty street corner, would get sicker to here the thoughts I thought in the last couple of weeks.

I drank bottle after bottle and slept fucking crazy. I sat on my couch long enough to drink some more and then fall asleep again. I did this over and over and over for weeks. I got Cocaine and paced silly paths in my apartment. I gnawed at my cheek and lost my keys.

This has been going on for years now, away from these two people, and I have done unimaginable things to myself and to those around me. I have kept paranoia in my pocket and read too many books. I have picked up random black people downtown and asked them to find me crack. I have tried to fight my friends and desperately held on to my dignity, leaving so little of it left to connect with. Things I have done are in the dictionary under: Alcoholic; or: Drug Addict.

My life is smoking with the squealing rubber of last second brakes. Imagery just isn't enough anymore; setting the scene is a nightmare.

Tomorrow all of it ends. I will be healed. I will be counseled and devastated, ready to live with the society I feel has failed me. I can't wait to feel whole and drink and drive with water. I have abstract thoughts of having my feet under me and no headaches, no lost sentiments or corrupted ideas. I can't wait to be fixed. I can picture the carpet in rehab with whitewashed walls and doctors with glasses getting me to speak about why I started drinking and who created the earth. Nurse's waiting for my call.

Today, I want to say goodbye to this couple, inform them that they don't have to worry about me. I love them. I sip my drink and leave. It is time to go.

2..

I am absolutely not qualified to tell you any of this. And, I base my opinions on no statistical or academic evaluations of any kind. This is not the linear tale of a gifted protagonist, this is how it feels to have no sense of agency.

I watched shows on recovery in between reading books. I feel as though the people I watch are a part of my extended family. In the weeks before deciding to go to rehab I saw a story about a man who drank himself homeless, cried in his coffee, and woke up to an intervention. A whole life between commercials. It took, and he lives normally with others who are trying to forget now. It reminded me of my own Moment, when I realized that I was sick in a way only sadistic, ready-made, bipolar teenagers could understand. Crying is compulsive, impulse control becomes fantasy, and hurting yourself is like eating lunch. With men like me there is no warning, no calling card for those I know. The downfall is abrupt and completely thorough. I don't start one night with a light beer, get drunk, play cards, and go home. I don't drink monotonously for weeks before it starts creating problems at work. It is immediate and I consume like I am trying to die. Work becomes a memory, my relationships become manic and indefinable, and my sense of morality is bubblegum.

My car drives itself into liquor store parking lots all of the time. I cannot understand that, I see my hands holding the wheel. I learned two very important things about myself before deciding to go to rehab: 1. I always whispered the things that mattered most, and yelled the things that mattered the least. And, 2. I was so messed up that after masturbation, I wanted my dick to leave.

I remember in the few weeks before rehab I was drinking, I was bingeing, waiting for the red sun, snorting Cocaine into a mess, rocking straight to not feel my heartbeat. I was waking up to whatever was left, pushing back withdrawal with whatever I had. I was into a pint by mid-morning because I knew it would make me feel a little bit better and by the afternoon I was racing. It was snowing every day; nosebleeds as appetizers. The problem was I had met my match.

Early on in my addiction I had a problem finding Cocaine and the people I tried to get it from were irreverent. They didn't care whether I got it and slid, or was turned away to drink over my disappointment. They didn't spend time bagging it and dressing it up. They were trying to make some extra money, not trying to ensure my medicine. The guy who I recently got it from was invested. He would deliver it to me, all I had to do was call and identify myself and he would just tell me how long it would be until he knocked on my door. He was a professional in the misery-delivery service and it worked to his advantage to bring it to me. The more I would do, the wider the spiral, and the more I would spend. At the end of my last binge I was hallucinating and not eating. I was going days without brushing my teeth and was telling my loved ones I was somebody else. I was driving drunk after two DUI's, living on the edge, over the edge, crying non-stop to the sounds of the modern. I couldn't quit, I couldn't even think of a way to get started on moving on. I was so complete. I was a host for a germ that has its own agenda.

  I had lost my job again, scared my imaginary companions, ignored my friends and laughed at my girlfriend. I had hate, I had thrown this time on the pile and added it to the hysteria. I was the master of the fucking universe.

  One week before all of that I was two days clear of my last bender, studying, as always. Living in the daylight, opposed to that vampire consuming in night. Life immediately after a binge, it is like eating a piece of exotic candy after spooning shit in to your mouth for a week. I was clear, I didn't feel wet inside or slippery in my stomach. I just felt the knock of what I had done or said the previous nightmare. After a time, you get so you binge just to feel the way you do the day after you withdrawal. Without despair, you never understand hope. I was reading *LENIN,* by Robert Service and I had just finished *CHE GUEVARA: A Revolutionary Life,* by Jon Lee Anderson. For the fourth time. I have a succession of ideas after I finish a book; a progressive contemporary development of what I believe to be the most applicable doctrines of any ideology or philosophy that I study. I wonder what in this complexity will be relevant to people today, and to what extent they will be willing to listen to someone who has smoked crack and slept in mud. To someone who has lost himself weary, and collected compliments from unknowing cab drivers.

  Originally, decades ago, I only wanted to be a part of a populist movement, in popular culture. Then, I wanted to be a part of a true revolution. Then, I realized that my pain would always exceed my imagination. Because sometimes I can feel the pulse of injustice, I can feel its roots and am not surprised as it blossoms. I can imagine these things, I can call to them, and then I am twist-to-the-top chapstick. Mechanical and useless. In one window, on a particular and powerful day as I was reading, I remember thinking that what I understand is important and that this impulse is not trivial.

I thought maybe I can write something comprehensive. Maybe I can learn and not collect random tragedy to put on paper; maybe I can make some sense and not be so fractured and difficult to understand.

I was thinking that after these books an ideological merging of some of the old-school psychological toughness and the modern intellectual creativity is what everyone in my generation needs. I was thinking that there needs to be a complete waging of suburban, intellectual guerrilla warfare. Contemporary American revolutions need not and cannot be violent, there is only room for or a necessity of elementary vanguards and philosophical and political and social and economic bullets and bombs. Foothill war with new ideas. Revolutions are everywhere.

There needs to be a reinvention at the University level and for this to translate to the public High Schools. We need to teach more about attitude, the approach we take to what we learn and how the subtext of what we study will be what is eventually passed on to the next thinking age. We need to forget the piece of cardstock paper with our names and titles at the end of the proverbial tunnel. The institution of the University, after all, is not just a collection of buildings, meetings, classes, and grades. Like Pirsig taught me, it is the advancement of thought and the perfection of technical specialization. I was thinking that currently there must be a separation in our minds of ourselves from those around us, because of the attitudes and interpretations I currently see on news TV. We need heroes. We need people who can keep at bay the incessant feelings of worthlessness and contradiction better than I can.

I was thinking that men my age are always impressed when they read about Che Guevara, or Steve Biko, or Malcolm X, or Bertrand Russell. And they are immortalized by the idea that they could be such men. Such men of courage and circumstance. The truth is, men now do not have the constitution, cultural commitment, or sacrificial depth of vision that the men I read about regularly exhibited. I remembered, that I don't know anyone who reads anything. And eventually, if the men here in my now are motivated to help change, they remember their apathy. Part of it is that the times have changed. The world has experienced, absolutely nothing less than, the periodical, pivotal Moment in human history. Global connectivity has information right at our fingertips, and knowledge in our wastebaskets. Economic exploitation has attained new levels of sophistication and poverty, hunger, and disease are still bedposts of our present. But there is still no unique historical context for our young people, the American youth, no cohesive unifying argument to wage our war with. Everyone is an expert, no one is a student, and there is always another cause. The technological revolution since my conception has only distanced us from each other. There is no distinct social movement, or radically moral war to identify with. We don't understand one another, and so we fear. The little wars that temporarily interrupt our entertainment are subservient to too many mediums. The bad news just isn't news anymore, it's just bad. Men are uninvolved, and helpless. Everything in the world has value only in that it may be used to distract us from our troubles. The Internet and the globalization of divisive resources have kept us fighting for the wrong things. Everything is homogenized and totally detached from actual reality.

This is form fitting, for no new heroes. At least not geographically relevant to shortsighted Americans. Wait for the Arab Spring to be over, then I will bleed with passion and be inspired, for once, by the present. I was thinking that something is going to bubble up and drip from my mouth if I don't stop it.

Learning in pieces is a resonating catharsis for all of us, if we so choose to indulge, so that we can abstain from new bigotry and regain our connection with the practicality of simple reason. These ideas come and have a finality I can see down the road. But, in all this, I was just thinking. My ideas were never thoroughly developed. I come close, to perfection, to feeling total. I read and engage myself socially, but lurking in the back, ready for the pounce, are my excuses. They come and go, just as I feel that I am on to something, they lie to me. They tell me that it will never get better, it will never go away. I can feel how disjointed all of this is, but I must tell someone. It could be right in the middle of something that fascinates me, then something tugs. Like this one day.

These were just ideas. I smoked a cigarette and congratulated myself on being so deep and beautiful. I got a bottle. I ended up in treatment a few weeks later.

3..

He will be my best friend in rehab. He is wearing a shirt that says: Rehab is for Quitters.
He says, "So, I'm fucking this guy in the ass, right? I figure screw it, so I go to give him a reach-around, and he has a hard-on, the fag!"

I laugh until I want to drink. Jokes in therapy are better therapy than therapy. They cool off your day and help you relax, and occasionally, introduce you to someone you will become very close with and trust completely. Laughter has been a stranger. You never laugh from the inside when you are drinking, you only giggle superficially. You do not have the perspective or the dedication to laugh at things deeply. You are so ashamed of what you have become and what monsters are haunting you that you feel laughter will be the cause of something catastrophic. Something that you will never be able to forget. So you don't do it.

The staff members here are to be purposely over-intrusive and confrontational but the other guys are there to catch you when you fall. They are there to be your mirror. Their stories vary and they all have experienced addiction at different levels of intensity, but they all, in some way or another, have walked across hot coals. They have all done what I have done, living shamefully, disgraced by the actions of someone too proud to admit when he's beat. Alcohol appeals to and cures any demographic on the planet, it is the pacifying butter we lay on our day and consume perpetually until we can't remember taste. It doesn't matter what part of the country you come from, what sort of socio-economic background you come from, what margin of violence you come from, what schools you come from, what Mother you come from, you can take this sip and all is healed. You can fix your boredom, fill your emptiness, and feed your hate.

This man, this joking funny man, is Greg. I hate his T-shirt and think it is stupid to wear the first day you are in treatment, you should wait until you know all of these guys a little bit better. They will know that you have made a commitment to recovery and that you are serious about a new life. They won't think you are an asshole. But I will soon know how he feels about the approval of other people. His accent is just as offensive. He is from Oklahoma, but sounds like the Deep South to me. His words draw out and tail off, but his sentences are quick. His ideas are complete, and it is refreshing to meet someone bright. Not that I haven't met anyone intelligent in rehab but I find something about him personally relatable. I see he carries pain. He does somehow speak slowly, but his thoughts are always finished. He has a point and it is usually inoffensive but hard. I really like him. And the fact that he started with a gay joke in which he was gay, that made me like him even more.

I have been here a week, and since I arrived, of course, this all seems premature. It seems as though I may have come here too soon, like this probably won't be effective. In the first week, you have time to adjust to not peeking out of your living room drapes, and shushing everyone in the living room to not alert the FBI. You get used to not knocking on liquor store doors to try to get them to open five minutes early because you are sick. When you walk into the front door of the treatment center you walk down, if you're not in a wheelchair, then you roll down the accessible ramp, and you find yourself in a sort of waiting area. It is tiled and has several small tables with a collection of lockers on the right. The nurse's station is on your left, where they go through all of your stuff to look for 'stuff.' It is invasive and symbolic of what you must prepare yourself for over the next 28 days. You are checked in there shortly after arriving and at some point you make your way across the small waiting area into the main room. Seven days after I have done this I have witnessed the repetition of my first day far too often. I have watched new men enter, run squealing and flailing. I have watched them stay and go forward. New guys that enter are wrapped in cellophane. And you can always see when they have that Moment. The Moment when someone realizes that the alcohol is gone. The party is over, and this was a huge mistake. I don't want to be here. I don't think that I need this. Every book about recovery on the planet has described this situation, but still, you will promise anyone anything just to go home. Every new student has this look on their face and this limp in their attitude. They don't belong here.

The main room is taken straight from a graphic novel. There are over twenty African animals, mounted on the wall, pissed off and smiling, staring at you in the center of their room. There is an elephant, a tiger, a cheetah, and a feeling like you can't possibly have walked into this place awake. This has to be a dream, it couldn't be any more cliché. Out with the old and in with the new. A reawakening, a new beginning. You will be raped with platitudes in this place. And the animals know it. They don't look afraid, like they had just gone for a walk and took a bullet in the ass. They look like they are grinning, because they are not you. They were just part of the natural, cyclical, evolution of the raw. They are not parasitic to society. This place actually used to belong to an accomplished hunter who used to store his women here in the mountains, away from the action, while he and his friends went on safari and mastered the manhood we all take for granted.

Across the desert you fall a few steps into an entry way and back up a few steps into the dining area. This is the only room in which you see the women who have come to get back their innocence. You eat with them and have one lecture each day with them, and that is definitely enough. They screech and laugh too loud and are constantly putting on a huge fucking production. I don't believe one of them has ever had a positive, worthwhile relationship with another woman in their entire lives. Given that women have such poor self-images to begin with, healthy in life and fat in the reflection, it is no wonder they don't need programs like this universally. I know everything.

The main building where we stay is surrounded by snow, paths lead to the cabins we all stay in after the required seventy-two hour waiting period. This is three days you need so you can be cleared medically, and they can tether your hopes to the comfort and warmth of the fireplace. So you think, 'Nah, I will run home tomorrow.' The property is away from anything meaningful, tucked in behind a smaller Colorado town. I had never heard of it before I went looking. There is a gazebo twenty feet from the main lodge where you walk to smoke cigarettes and take breaks in between meetings.

After you are through with the ransack at the nurse's station, you are introduced to your sponsor. He is to be your introduction to the brave new world, the first sober gathering you may have attended in years. He means that you are not going to party ever again and that your lies have been broadcasted in High-Definition. He shows you around, walks you through the rules and the schedule. The rules dictate that you will be obedient and organized, but also that you will be unashamed and unapologetic. He is perfectly chokeable.

At your first meal your sponsor taps his drinking glass with a spoon or fork and stands up to introduce you to everyone: "Everyone, I would like to welcome Jay." And then there is applause and you feel corny. Formal logic won't help you here. It reminded me of Malcolm X, who believed that the first step of any successful rehabilitation program was to get the afflicted to believe that he is worthy of recovery and that it is a real possibility. But in this room full of strangers, people are staring at you, and this probably hasn't happened since you had the pipe, and the others thought you were taking too long with it.

Then he introduces you to everyone, one by one, and they all smile at you like they have something important figured out. I wanted to punch every last one of them. Then, depending on what time of day you arrive, you make your first meeting, or eat your first meal. Half of the ten thousand dollars you have to pay must go directly to the kitchen staff. The food is excellent, salad bar second to none, and if you're bulimic, you are going to have your work cut out for you. If you go to a meeting first, then pity on you. It is strange to walk in to a room of people constantly speaking about how horribly they feel, remembering some of the things they've done, and crying to feel better. Men touching each other and smiling. Guys telling guys that they care, giving each other and themselves affirmations. Licking each other's wounds. Especially considering everyone in your life, and you, has spent the last part of any meaningful time completely ignoring the huge cancer on your face. From six-thirty in the morning until ten o'clock at night they have you doing something groundbreaking and totally cathartic.

I doubt the schedule really appeals to the surfer, nihilist demographic. It is regimented and you are noticed if you are gone. Part of others' recovery, apparently, is to make sure that you are where you're supposed to be. Some students will make it a career in rehab to call every other addict on their "bullshit." The "bullshit" we all have pulled over the eyes of the world for so long. In my head I call every one of these people Mom. Mom is nice, she is generous. But maybe too generous. Too willing to get involved in your life and point out the insufficiencies and incongruities. Parody has done her to death, but she is the marker. She is the most overbearing and over-concerned person in your life. Not my Mom, but maybe yours. She is your involved, co-dependant Mom, still ringing your ears with: "Be careful." She can be a real bitch.

This particular treatment center refers to its addicts as students. Not clients, patients, or fucking maniacs. Students, because they want you to feel as though you are here to learn and you are not just a paycheck. Students because the relationship you have with your counselor will be professorial and academic. It will be professional and directed toward the specific goal of your recovery. It won't be negotiation. Secretly, the counselors and technicians, the immature and not fully evolved ones, along with the nosy and 'too concerned with your problems so I don't have to deal with my own' Moms, will make you feel like a client by helping you understand conformity. By assuring your obedience, by always cocking their heads with concern, they will make sure that you know you make others sad. They will exhaust themselves with anecdotes on how your bad language has set the standard for your life, and how you need to use words with care so you don't get out of rehab and use again. They assault you with reasons on how public behavior, especially in the presence of family members who are visiting and young people, is the gateway to private contentment. They make you puke in the toilet. They put you through reformatory school for adults, they give you cup-holders for your hate and suitcases for your insults.

If at the end of this process, your first full week, the introduction and inoculation, the angelic merging of your physical withdrawal and the beginning of a clearly better life, the first day of the rest of your death, you can lie down in bed and peacefully go to sleep, you need to drink more.

4..

During drinking, whether a lightly righteous period, or a strikingly heavy psychotic breakdown, time and space collapse on themselves. You have no awareness or registration of chronology or distance. We have all seen the external stumbling, but internally it is exponentially worse. Speed and size of physical objects and internal bio-functioning are chaos. Everything becomes an oil painting with images and colors blending into a neurological kaleidoscope. The world seems different when you're not producing new memories. You can wake up, snap to, temporally reconstruct, in the middle of a blackout and not know what you're doing. I heard of a guy who had this happen to him during sex. He was having sex like animals have sex, he couldn't see her face, and he was suddenly present. Restored to consciousness. His heart didn't pound with fear and his hopes weren't for world peace, he only asked one pervading question, "Who in the hell am I having sex with right now?" I have awoken driving, playing sports, going on break at work. My body is functioning and I am performing habitual acts of normal life. I am eating, showering, going to places, but I am not ever present. The major part of my brain that records and analyzes the day-to-day occurrences in my psychological memory bank has gone to a party. But you don't realize this until you have your awakening. Suddenly you can feel your extremities, you are aware that you don't feel well. You momentarily understand that you have been absent for a period of time. Who knows how long it has been. Who knows what you have done, but you are back now, and it is an exciting, sub-human realization that you never want to recreate.

    Alcoholism will make you a scientist. Everything is relative. The theory of Special Relativity stipulates that time and space are not absolute, they change, they warp, and they are specific to each observer who is in relative motion to another observer at constant velocity. This not only applies to the movement of planets or to the speed at which objects travel in the universe in relation to bodies of mass and gravity, but also to the common human experience. For instance, if you have a friend who is an asshole, but his Father is a bigger asshole, then your friend will not seem like so much of an asshole when you spend time with them both simultaneously. Time that extends infinitely, where a minute is an hour and an hour is a death sentence. Or, if you meet a girl during a blackout and suddenly become fully conscious in the middle of sexual intercourse, she can't be any worse looking than women in your ugliest addict dreams.

The inviolable laws of nature are always in my mind, in my heart. I feel so powerfully about their simplicity and beauty, sometimes they are all that saves me from jumping off of the edge. As long as I am talking about them, I am not dying.

The fundamental principle of relativity is ubiquitous in all of our daily lives but few of us explore its origins or its intellectual ramifications. Ordinary people, to my knowledge, are not concerned with the subtleties of life. They do not seem to require particular intellectual satisfaction or maturation in areas like Philosophy, Religion, Science, Mathematics, History, Art, or Literature. Maybe not intravenously injecting poison into your body allows you to worry about what is practical for yourself and your family. Maybe it is their indifference that allows them to breathe.

A month before I went to rehab I read *Einstein: A Life*, by Denis Brian. It immediately made sense to me because of what transpired in my addiction. I went to meet my dealer for the fourth day in a row to get more Cocaine and got a balloon to bring home. This is not an isolated period, finding a source, unique to this late stage in my addiction. This has been the case since the beginning of my troubles. My dealer only dealt until seven o'clock at night. Satan with a schedule. I got home, sweating with the excitement of anticipation, heart and bowels on fire, and opened the balloon to find heroin. I hadn't done heroin in a long time but there was no getting a hold of him to make an exchange. I cut it up and snorted. Contrary to the persistent public opinion of heroin where the addict slows and drools, nodding to the movement-rhythm of his discontent, I just slept. I slept like I hadn't in days and dreamt of Nyquil. I slept through phone calls and alarms, through terrible dreams, and tugging at my shirt. I slept like I never wanted to stop.

When I awoke, Cocaine was *relatively* harmless. Only because of the social stigma that attributes heroin to needles and needles to aids. Needles to alleyways and jaundiced skin with junkies and ghettos. Aids with gays and the destruction of marriage, gays with the tendencies of sexual promiscuity and deviant exploration. The horrific visualization of dope fiends and basements, the affiliation of white-pasted lips and someone who will seemingly do absolutely anything to get the next fix.

Heroin is ugly and slow. It is an opiate and blurs your speaking and makes you feel like a baby. People cannot stand to be around a heroin addict.

Cocaine, inexplicably, still has a distant relationship to highbrow nightclubs and sensational parties. People still get a hell of a lot of work done on Cocaine. People are tolerable because they still pay their bills. Until the late stages of Cocaine addiction, the addict has to function somewhat normally to obtain more Cocaine. In the national portrait, Cocaine is still the expensive leather ottoman. It has crowded us and depreciates the value of the room, but we all know it isn't going anywhere. It is not what has come to be known as the cultural thorn and abrasive, poor people anesthetic that is crack. (Don't even get me started on Crystal Meth, because I may never stop.) Cocaine costs money and ends with expensive palm resorts. Crack causes incestual rape and record high twentieth century murders. For someone like me, talking of the distinction between crack and traditional Cocaine is a sociological exercise. Like, should we eat cardboard or wood? It is deciding whether to blame the rampaging serial killer, or his parents. People are dead no matter what.

With the heroin, my vacation is over. Time and space, because of sleep, regain their calm and specific interaction. They again have continuity and sensible definitions. And now I really am a nasty addict. Relativity now has a distinct meaning, only it has me defined as someone completely out of control.

After this episode though, and the sweet taste of candy, I actually feel like I have a more personal relationship with science. It is not abstract or marginal, it is something I need to fall in love with. Thank you heroin. If scientific practice is truly only objective and observational there is really no need for its existence, funding, or application. That definition excludes it from, and is antithetical to, the basic tenets of experimentation. The hypothesis and requisite proof continue to assist us in helping the fulfillment of our understanding of our environment. They help us know. If they were ambivalent motivations, humanity would not need to engage in their development. All of it now has a lot to do with me. Theoretical physics has something to do with me being alive. If I did not barely comprehend relativity, I wouldn't have known how bad my life was, or how it still wasn't as bad as death. Or that I still had lots of time left, and any time spent sober from here on will be absolutely, perpetually better than what I had observed. I would not have known that compared to regular people, stupid and irrelevant, my life had become totally unlivable. I would not have known that the whole universe was created for me to exist.

After all, we are not just a collection of cells, molecules, gases, transmitters, frequencies, neurons, and electricity. We also carry with us the capacity to laugh and love, the constitution for the projection and development of better ideas, and the intellectual potential to understand our own extinction and how that will affect the rest of time. Addicts personify the separation between mental capacity and physical functioning.

The state I find myself in after doing Cocaine like that and ending up the episode with heroin is somewhat curious. I know that my life is miserable, that it has no future, that I am killing myself. But, paradoxically, all of the pain that exists within me and in the world at large is all I have. Because I have never felt a part of the whole. Because I have never understood what drives other, normal people. Because I don't understand the motivation for war. Because I, once and ultimately, hated my Father. Because everyone mistreats me and no one cares. Because I am an artist. Because, if the world or I were perfect, art and entertainment would not exist as mediums. Perhaps, because I have never bothered to notice anything else at all.

Because, this is all really annoying.

5..

I am bent to the floor and walking too much. I am a little bit restless because on your tenth day, you have to do your 'first step.' Of the famous twelve. It reads:

1. We admitted to ourselves that we were powerless over alcohol and that our lives had become unmanageable.

My first step is tomorrow, my tenth day. In the ritual that becomes your each day you usually witness two things: A first step; and a peer evaluation. The first step is monumental, it is where you tell your story. You begin with your childhood. You touch on what your youth was like, if your parents were addicts, and what affect this may have had on your eventual using. You move on to being a teenager and the first time you experimented with drugs or alcohol. The first time you considered jumping off of a high-rise, and the last time you ever felt like a normal human being. Eventually, you have to get to your transformation. When did you start drinking in the early morning? When did you begin, if you have them, ignoring and abusing your kids? When did you start masturbating to women in your family? When did you first end up in jail? When did you start lying to everyone? When did you become a calculating, cannibalistic consumer? When did you lose all enthusiasm and fuck caution to the wind? How did you end up here?

Some of the first steps are moving. They are done in an isolated room with the members of your group. The center splits the men into two groups, Group C and Group D. There are too many drags to keep together at once. Some of the first steps are intense and communicable. They consume you and you know you are not alone. I have seen these. They make me sad and remind me of the fact that I am not unique. The poignant stories are made up of a wicked humor and a total loss of humanity. The ones that I gravitate towards make me feel like I have a brother and are a reflection of the way I have felt. They are reciprocity. The tales that I have told and lived articulated by someone else.

The other ones are pathetically boring. The other people have not drank or used nearly enough to be entertaining to me. There is something insincere about the way they tell their story. Something in it sounds as if it is made up, something doesn't quite sound right. They are devoid of personal responsibility and exaggerated self-loathing. They don't hate themselves as much as they should. It has always been someone else. The drinking and lazy suicide are a product of the treatment one has received as a special person just trying to make their mark. These are the men who I will not become close with. Whether a factual distance splitting us by two different, too different stories, or the simple inability to convey their pain, we come to an impasse. It doesn't matter to me, I will not connect with the people who haven't collapsed in grief.

Then, the day after you do your first step, the peer evaluation. After you listen to a first step you must immediately recite the Serenity Prayer and then go to the main room to fill out a 'Peer Evaluation' worksheet. On the front is a list of character defects. A range of characteristics you have employed or simply acquired to deflect responsibility and minimize the effects that your using has had on those that love you. They are numbered and explained and you must check at least three that the 'first-stepper' has personified. On the back are lines to write on and you have to diagnose the symptoms of this particular addict. Then, after dinner, sometimes you engage in a fun-forgetting hour of board games, usually an AA meeting, a 'nightly reflection,' and you go to bed. You wake up and in mid-morning your group surrounds the guy who did his first step the previous day. You give him a chair that rolls, sit around him in a horseshoe, and read him the 'peer evaluation' worksheet that you have completed dutifully.

He rolls towards you and you extend your hand. You clasp like he is dangling from the edge of a cliff, and you're Tom Cruise, holding him in the balance. You clasp your hands like you are getting ready to arm wrestle. You tell him what items on the front of the sheet you have selected, how he is totally fragmented and disfigured. Then you read what you wrote on the back. One could go like this:

> *Max,*
> *I like the way you told your story. It was fucked up what your Dad did to you when you were young. Your Mom doesn't sound very nice either. It must be hard to deal with the death of your sister last year. But you were never even there for her anyway! All you have ever done is run from your problems and drank yourself to death! How does it feel to know that your kids hate you? How do you think your parents feel to have a drunk as a son? How does your wife feel that you can't even hold down a*

job? I hope you get all of this together because you are a nice person.

Love,
Whoever.

Then you list something additional that you think will be helpful to their recovery and three positive attributes they have as people. This is not hard, these are just people. Though, sometimes, it is like talking about the superb organization of the Nazi party. You then, as a group, write for them a 'meal statement', which is usually in poetic form, that they have to read during a meal, in front of everyone. It is self-deprecating and about their usage.

The peer evaluation is obviously harder than someone's first step. In the first step you are an impartial observer, witness to the hanging. In the peer evaluation, you are a participant. A lethal injector. You don't want to hurt anyone's feelings but they need to hear this. I have a hard time doing these because I have never liked feeling like a hypocrite. How can I tell someone else how wrong and slippery he is when I feel like the worst? It is also counterintuitive to me. I am not here to comment on the failings and disgusting behavior of other men like me, but to focus and interpret the results of my own addiction. Later, I realize that this is a conditioning to help you recognize that your most miserable of deeds, your most grotesque actions, are common to people who have carried with them the disease and the resulting guilt. Helping others is helping your self. You are all ugly, not just him. I should not have thought that they were boring, because I am boring.

With the impending status of my first step I review my history. I recall my feelings and go through my actions from childhood, to adolescence, to young adulthood, and superstar of professional alcoholic in training. I must speak about coming to rehab, the reasons and enraging collection of devious, behavioral imperfections. I have to tell the people I now care about, adore, and respect, how I was a week a way from killing one of them. I don't like it. I don't like its thickness.

I have gotten close to people in here. On TV I watch reality shows. I would watch people cry and spill together, and tell each other 'I love you,' after living together for two weeks. I wanted to puke. I thought that there was no possible way you could actually love someone after such a short period of time. You couldn't feel about them the way you have felt about others you have cared for. But I was wrong. Not only is there an abundance of physical proximity to these men but also there is an emotional chord we all play simultaneously. We have all been Mickey-Mouse fairytales, and bad-guy chameleons. He has done what I have done, and I have done what he thinks funny. There are several people in here that I love. And will love absolutely when I leave.

There is a young cat, Superman, the most mature eighteen-year-old I have ever been around. He is built like a football star and carries a disposition like Clint Eastwood. He is good-looking and has a huge sense of humor. He laughs at me, and I love him for it. He was strung out on OxyContin. He had compromised everything positive in his life for eighty milligrams a day. His lows were low, breaking up and snorting to have his brother walk in, and his high was fun. It just got to be too much. He began stealing and lying. Something that, after knowing him for a short time, I know has him reeling. He isn't a thief, and has no desire to be a politician.

There is a smaller guy, as nice as Gandhi. Good looking, very welcoming. Unassuming and quiet. He is Nick. He sits on the couch in the main room when we are all there, in all our glory, relating stories of our hideous days. He observes impartially, and seems to soak it all in. When he speaks he tilts his forehead forward and mumbles at the ground. He is sharp and fucked-up. I think he has always felt that he couldn't measure up. That his parents were too good, his brother was God, and that he shouldn't be. I think he has constantly tied himself to people not worth his time, and is, like me, severely physically and spiritually addicted. He has told me about month-long binges, hiding in his fix, visiting his parents' house at times he knows he will be alone to shower and get right. His attitude sometimes borders on somber but he is always ready to laugh. He scarcely said a word the first week he was here. One day we are out in the gazebo, and up comes a mouth with legs. Greg is all ready to tell us how he talks too much. He tells us to let him know. He gets half of the way through a story and Nick leans over, quiet and unassuming, "You know we would get along a lot better if you would just shut the fuck up."

I think Nick is pure, and beautiful.

Greg is most like me, and this is my crew. The people who have been hazed by life and came out a bit jaded, but still hopeful. Greg falls down hard. Weeks before he came to rehab he was mad. He was mad and decided to do something about it. He got in his truck and drove to a gun store. He got back in his truck and headed east out of Oklahoma City, Oklahoma. He drove to Memphis, shooting road signs with a thirty-eight. When you run you run fast and with a purpose. You run to prove a point, and goddamn it if you aren't going to show everyone what you are capable of. He drove up to a black man in Memphis and tried to buy drugs. He specifically directed this black man to get him Cocaine, not crack. The man met his thirty-eight and walked away with no money after bringing back rocks.

Greg, the funny accountant, the homegrown stud, drove to Key West via Memphis smoking crack the whole way. Greg has a spider-web in his brain, he catches people with charisma and eats them alive. He "vacations" in Florida for a few days with Cocaine, alcohol, and Xanax. He has a business meeting to go to in Philadelphia in a week. Which he attempts to include his body in. The problem is, the day before the meeting is his birthday and the third day of an idealists binge. When he arrives he crunches beetles in his teeth and screams paranoia. He sets up at an airport hotel and after a marathon becomes settled. He makes it to the meeting ready for a fight. Glowing like a toy with his eyes like a fountain. He is dismissed from the meeting, red and sweating, and goes to his hotel room. At some point he becomes convinced that down the hall, in the rooms adjacent and next to his, are people he knows. He believes that the people he cares for are going to set him up.

The Intervention is a tenuous plan. There are results that vary in success just like any other plan, but with an intervention a life is close to ending. If it is too soon, the addicted will run or resent, bury his head in the dirt and search for answers. He will be very mad and it may drive him to do things that have been worse than previous actions. He may go mad, and go alone. On the other hand if it is just at the right time, it may save a life. When someone has lost all hope, looked for results in every corner, and truly feels that there are no other options to consider, he will give rehab a real shot and respect the people he loves for doing it. If it is too late, you are probably gathering for a funeral anyway. Intervention is overtime; the game, in the eyes of those that have been watching, is over, one big mistake means you lose. So be careful and conscious before you think of an intervention.

Greg flushes his Cocaine in Philadelphia and goes running down to the airport, scaring people waiting to go visit. He is wearing an orange shirt and is convinced that people are chasing him. He tears off his shirt and throws it away in the terminal. He takes his wallet and throws it to the masses. He runs miles to the police station, shirtless and without identification, the last place I would want to end up, and tells them his state of emergency. He could have just said he killed Kennedy. He is told, to my fucking astonishment, to go back to his hotel. His Mother is contacted and ends up going to the hotel he is at. Flying in for the rescue. He leaves his wife, stepdaughter, and daughter wanting as he comes to treatment. His peer evaluation was comedy, and unfathomably sad.

My first step is tomorrow. My last step seems always. My feet sort of tremble, and I am absolutely ready to tell all these men how broken I am. I am ready to liberate myself and start fresh. I want to tell them what I have done, what not to do, and what formative years I absolutely cannot remember.

6..

Months before my entrance into the alive, my Dad is the coolest.
He says, "What happened, bud?"
"You will only need one guess," I say.
We have been through this so many times. This is not a happy time in my life. Hot, never-ending summer. I can't seem to get kicked out of my apartment. I can't seem to lose any friends. I can't seem to get my third DUI. This is not without effort. At one point I am driving totally wrecked, subservient to the rubber bands I use as legs. I come over a hill in my neighborhood speeding and taking a big, calming drink of vodka. I am pulled over, sure my breath smells like medicine, ready for the wrist-steel. I am not really nervous but resigned to the fact that I probably will be going to jail, and spending a lot of time there before it is all done. I get a seat-belt citation with a fine and follow the rainbow to the golden pot of miraculous treasure. My Mom knew about this because she was there, I never told my Dad.

My Mom and Dad have had the same run with me, basically. But my Mom is also an addict. I am not sure how she would feel about me writing this, but to me it is clear. She is very kind, she cares about people, she wants to help in some way. But she drinks all of the time. I free-based with her a lot over the last couple of years and I could talk for days about the psychological ramifications of using drugs with your parents, and then say 'that is probably bullshit.' The truth is that it hurts. It is one thing to look in the mirror, to look at yourself and not believe that this is what you are. But to see someone who raised you in the same condition: Mentally unclear and confused. Emotionally starved and immature. Professionally lost. It is so so sad.

She has always been there for me, told me that I am great and that I have things to offer and not to give up, I thinks she thinks that I am the reason she was put here. I recognize in her a dream to be better, but no energy to act. It is so so sad, and I love her so much. I have done unimaginable things in her presence and she has always been there to tell me it is okay. But seeing her is sometimes pain, suitable for my destruction. In a way, she is the only reason I am able to understand the people in my life, the way they deal and cry with me. My Dad is different.

My Dad recently told me what summarized his attitude. His nurturing disposition and supportive demeanor. He is always ready to listen to my story, to tell me I am human, and to give me a job. He is never condescending or paternalistic anymore. He wasn't always this way but as I have transgressed, he has transformed, and never lets me off the phone without telling me he cares. He said that because of his Father he knew that there was only one thing he could do. His father beat him frequently, and drank from morning to night. He never has had a real problem with alcohol, though he tells me he is also an alcoholic. I think to make me feel better. He said he knew that all of my drinking was totally out of his control, that he was completely powerless. He told me the only thing that he felt that he could do was to make sure that I knew I was loved. He told me that he hated what I was doing, he didn't hate me. Satellites don't experience perspective like this. I have no doubt that if half of the people in rehab were the recipients of this kind of sincerity, they would have a chance. But much more than half of them don't.

There is no way to overstate how important paternal support is for a boy. Your Father is a model for god, he is absolutely the impression you get of perfection when you are young. His attention is all you want and his approval is something you will seek for at least the first third of your life. He is strong and never scared. In my desperation, I needed him so badly, and he was there. I would like to think that I don't need anyone, that I am smart enough and strong enough and the people I read about will save me. I like to think that my Will is the epitome of Nietzsche, and that every person on earth would be jealous. But the truth is, when I am using I am a scared little boy. I am cowering and cold and just want my parents to save me. And they did, in their different ways, they did.

If you are looking for underlying reasons why someone young began or persists using, even at the cost of their own life, the first place you should look (always) is to the nature and structure of their relationship with their parents. And for some reason, especially with their Fathers.

I have been in and out of coherence the entire summer. I live on my own now and have no one egging me to bend straight. To live well. They are all shut off by a red button on my cell-phone. All of their advice and encouragement drop to the bottom of the well, and they are submerged by an ocean of alcohol. It isn't that they don't matter, but I am gone. I am in the middle of a stretch where a pint will be breakfast and crack a side dish. It lasts an average of eight days, days I have evidently spent in part at my girlfriend's house, that I cannot remember. It lasts forever and is sporadic. It lasts and lasts and fucking lasts. Things are getting out of control. Of course, I attempt to keep this from everyone.

I am consuming more for longer periods of time again. I am spending money I do not have and coming to in reliable debt. I drink so much that I withdrawal too hard. I should be committed. I am having homosexual encounters with my friends, in my dreams. I am having unreasonable and completely unexpected racist thoughts. Especially about white people. I am experiencing new physical pain each day and am crying and dying. I am cutting myself, getting smooth blood on my clothes. I am showing up at places with no reasonable explanation. I get fired from a job, far from the first time, for smelling like alcohol.

I was sent home and I told them how hard of a time I was having. There were things they didn't know about, I told them. Problems with my family, they probably wouldn't understand, I said. They bought it outright at face value only to have me taking drinks in a stall in the bathroom one week later. These poor Judas'. They were actually going to bring me back again, but when I was sent home, I got lost in oblivion. I was totally saturated and didn't stop for another week.

For some reason, one that I imagine I will never fully have a good grip on, I persist in cutting myself. My sister has done this before inside of her own battles and I have never understood why she did this. But I started. I take out my pocketknife and I cut the backs of my hands, the backs of my forearms and my wrists. Never hard enough to warrant stitches or real medical attention but definitely enough to draw blood. A lot of blood, dripping down my arm onto my clothes and my furniture. I believe, after it is all over and I have the benefit of retrospect, that I want pain. I want to be fucking nasty, to appear worthless so that it is internally consistent. I want simply to see my own blood, and hopefully someone else will see it and I gain some pathetic affection. Soberly, all of these sentiments are very foreign to me, but I know that with depressants and stimulants fraternizing randomly in my systems at long enough intervals, the man that I call me is replaced by an immature, insignificant adolescent. You would not be speaking to the same person, I am not a cutter, you would be dealing with a psychopath.

I have read all about the neurological, psychological, and biological effects and consequences that come from using so much. But you can't feel that at the time, you can't understand how you have gone from such a good place to wasting away, grasping and tugging to try to take anyone down with you. I have no definitions for my relationships, there are no boundaries when I am using and nothing I won't do. This is a clear representation for me of the power of substance. Aristotle would be proud. It will be after me. I am at its mercy. When I get enough in me, people have called it the 'crossover.' When the person you know is gone and hidden and layered and beleaguered. And all that is left is a marginally functioning body with malfunctioning neurotransmitters and imbalanced chemistry. A miswired organism. That is me half of the time, crossed over. Gone. I am the night of the living dead.

I am narcoleptic and have insomnia. I am wishing for a personal tragedy so I can be excused for washing myself away. I am in a constant state of embarrassment, I am mentally weak. I am emotionally pathetic. I am operating primitively. I can't seem to catch up with how fast things move around me. People want me to get up and get going, to do something positive to get the ball rolling. People catch me sober and feel my sense of wonder, they hear my imagination shine out of my mouth, they see the complex wisdom and immature passion, and they are disgusted by my actions. They don't understand.

People say "cheer up" and "hang in there buddy" and "don't be so cynical" and I think: that is a fantasy. If you look any deeper than what is in your immediate surroundings the world is filled with poverty, disease, and hatred. And it saddens me to the core. It shakes my being.

People just don't get it. They want to, or not, but they don't. Unlike the first perfect drink I take at the start of a binge, where, I admit, I maintain total choice, deep in a binge my body won't function anymore. I am scared and startled by every insignificant change in my environment. My brain feels dense; it is hard. It feels like there are air pockets in it. There is information and courage that I can't access. My hands, feet, and face tingle in the absence of a functioning circulatory system. I am maniacally nervous. I speed with my vision from here to there taking no account of depth and shadow. Pity me, and hand me the world. I can't take a shower and pay my bills. I cannot confront what I have done.

I cry at everything and melt into movies. I have no understanding of my reflexive emotions. I cannot put sentences together or conduct myself with the slightest touch of humor. I look at the man in the mirror and see someone disfigured and hideous. I am not him, I can't be. I am totally in denial about what I have said to people and conclude that this is how it will be. It is just going to be like this, fine for a day or four at a time, then without warning, spinning too fast. Consuming like a garbage truck. Radiating ether. This sucks but there is no way out. I am dressing indifferently and not shaving for weeks so I look like a drummer. I am spitting on the carpet in my apartment and hating everything inside everyone. I run through people. And poor women.

Women have always had a thing for me. And I have run through them. I have tried to be respectful, but never understood the concept. I never really understood the complexity of a meaningful relationship with someone of the opposite sex, and drugs just compound the translation. I never saw a functional, positive date growing up. I gain access to the courage and love that women store in them somewhere by being charming and funny and smart, and I take it. I take all that they have saved for themselves. I find it easy to meet women, to talk to them and be nice to them, but real commitment and compassion are foreign to me.

At the end of a tired day, when you feel you have nothing left, reach down and do for your woman what you wouldn't even do for yourself. Do it for me. Do things for her that help her understand that you listen. Not listen, but *listen.* Listen to her, really, and find what she wants, what she is afraid of, what makes her smile on the inside, and never let her out of the room without telling her how beautiful she is. I know it's ridiculous, but so is not doing it.

Let these truths wash through you, and believe in your love with her, and touch her with your soul. Do not imagine the physical image of reaching out and actually touching her. Imagine closing your eyes, and having her just understand what she means to you. You can give her that every day, protect and support her, encourage and love her, listen and talk with her. You can remotely contribute to my protective feelings for females and help me salve my conscience. Or go get a needle, and come find me and we will be alone together. Because I have never done any of these things, and women still want me.

I am considering being gay. Latching on to something that will inherently force me to feel inferior and incomplete in a social paradigm. Something that will destroy me enough to make me not have to drink anymore. So that I don't have to do so many drugs. My god, so many drugs. Homosexuality itself has never personally appealed to me, I am too attracted to women. But there does seem to be an internal struggle in homosexuals familiar to the obsolete and common to previous segments of the global community experienced in the fight for equal rights. It is all very real. Black knots in the belly and desires of just being treated decently. I have gay dreams, and want the pain. There must be a huge feeling of isolation. It must be somewhat like being an alcoholic.

It never struck me as anything that had to do with choice. It is a physiological and bio-chemical production of specific hormones. So I am fucked. Alcoholics also have this, but gay people don't mumble and stutter their way through business meetings waiting to sneak for their next fix. Or maybe they do, I don't know. Homosexuality, to my way of thinking, is simply an occurrence in biological functionality. The physical presentation and emotional make-up of people they look to share time with is just slightly different from heterosexuals. They choose to be attracted to their own sexes no more than I choose to be attracted to women, it just is. What excites them physically is different, that is all. It is ridiculous to me the way they are treated all of the time.

Picture a man. A man with specific interests and unpopular needs. He goes to his parents and tells them that he is different, that his needs seem to be objective and created by something inside of him, something he doesn't really understand. After telling his parents of this need, they disown him. They tell him to get out and never come back, to consider himself alone and orphaned. Somewhere in the mess that is life he finds someone whose needs coincide with his. He finds someone, against all common sense for every last one of us, who embodies what is exciting to him and spiritually recognizable, and he feels safe and inspired with this person. Say this person is another man. He has a similar story and they both know that it is just the two of them. There is no parental help or supportive siblings. One of them gets sick. Sicker than sick and they know they will need to say goodbye. After all of this time, this man cannot make any medical decisions for his Other. He cannot delegate to the nurses that his partner is not to be resuscitated, he is in too much pain. Decisions that are automatically afforded to married couples. Decisions that will have an impact on the tone of the lives affected, and the atmospheric chemistry on earth for the rest of eternity.

The parents of either of these poor men are contacted, and, after not including this person in any part of their lives for any amount of time, get to arrive at the hospital and make completely ignorant, selfish, and detached decisions. This should make us all vomit like bile-saving alcoholics. These two states have to have similarities, alcoholism and sexuality. How poetic it all is, the illogical fear, the anecdotal storytelling. The absolute impotence in whining about it all.

If the next logical step after marriage for homosexuals is then the marriage of people to animals, I say where is the KY?

I can only imagine the part where the homosexual feels like part of the problem. I always believed that democracy is supposed to be about the freedom to argue the merit and validity of new ideas that are in opposition to each other and then come to the most inclusive, logical conclusion. Not the declaration of normalcy and the subsequent punishment for those on the outside. We are failing our brothers and sisters.

As alcoholics, I believe we do identify with this. I pointlessly explore it. I've always thought that anyone who is absolutely happy is devoid of meaningful expectations. As a human being, I never understood how you could be happy with the continued suffering of people so close to our hearts. This is where we all get along. I am an idealist, I am miserable and so are you and so are they. In *Why I Am Not A Christian* by Bertrand Russell, he speaks of sexual freedom and our need to recognize personal physical privacy. He speaks of the ridiculousness of common morality. I try to contrast it with my 'self', but forget what I have forgotten from him. I am trading my sense of morality and community for the medicine that keeps me sick, and makes me feel better. I am leeching off of society. I am rotting teeth and un-coagulated blood. I *am* hyperventilation. These people are just people, just different.

I didn't know that months after these revelations I would be in rehab, letting all of this sink in. I couldn't see that death was in the store, waiting for me to pay. I didn't know that these sensible ideas and horrific exploitations of my body wouldn't end abruptly. I am the liberal tyranny of all my cells. I am constantly drunk and high.

7..

I am a little nervous about my first step. It feels like my Iwo Jima. I do have protection but I am going to hang everything out there, unprotected, and hope as much comes back with me as possible. We always have them in the afternoon and all day people are asking you if you're ready. Like I am getting ready to go to a pageant or something. I am in the locker room getting ready for the big game, you know, pumping up and bumping chests. But there is no victory here. At least outwardly there is no group of beneficiaries or cheering crowds, but there is catharsis. I am sitting in the main room and going over in my head what I want to say, what I would want to tell my kids if I survive long enough to have any. Ten minutes until the almighty rains thunderbolts…I panic. I don't want to tell these people what I have done or how I feel. I don't want anyone to know how scared I have been or how much I have cheated everything and everyone stupid enough to entrust me with important parts of their lives. I don't want this. I am not really sure when all of that happened, I used to be as cool as the other side of the pillow. But now, now it feels as though I am nervous or anxious or overly cautious all of the time. I am always jittery and-

"Ready, Jay?"

The good thing about me is that I can muster courage when I have no reason to. My group and I get up all together and go to the stairs in a back hallway away from the main room in the 'lodge.' We walk up them and turn left into a conference room, past the intake call center. The call center is where the people sit, and judge, when you initially call to investigate whether or not this is something you will be interested in. They are all very nice and must lead very interesting lives. Pass their room and you are then in the conference room, a meeting room. When you walk in to your left is a counter with a coffee machine, microwave, sink, and small refrigerator. In the middle of the room is a table, a generous table surface for the elbows of people deciding to let someone live, or not. When people break the rules, this is where Yoda sits to understand what the motivation was, and if the student should be asked to leave.

Apparently, people are asked to leave for all sorts of reasons. Just before I came someone was kicked out of rehab for having prescription pills sent to him at the front desk. Wicked smart. Other people have been kicked out for poor attitudes, or for some discrepancy in the compensation the center receives for handing you back your soul. I imagine the most people who have been asked to leave have been asked to do so because of relationships with people of the opposite sex. They sneak off into the woods, or slip into the laundry room and become whole and complete and totally excited, at least for a period of time. To some it may feel as though this is another example of addicts lacking any capacity to follow rules, and to a certain extent in a lot of cases, this is probably true. It is also about a connection with someone. Someone else you are physically attracted to going through the same thing you are, someone who may be as devastated and broken. It is probably magnetic.

    I get ready to tell my story in the formal business setting.

    About a week after I got here someone from my group had to go to Court one morning in a city about forty-five minutes away from the center. He was able to get a ride the night before and was allowed to stay somewhere he thought was safe, attend his court date, and come back the following day. He relapsed the night he left and ended up in Detox. Because that is what we do. We have a bad night, I have a bad night, and I end up doing Heroin and laughing at suicide. I end up in jail or ruin a relationship completely or end up in the hospital because of some hideous, arbitrary injury. I don't drink at family functions too much and call my family names. I stay up for days and imagine not paying my bills, ever again. The guy that left, this charismatic, good-looking, really funny, crazily addicted guy, was allowed to stay. So you never know. You either get the guillotine or are anointed prince and given the kingdom. The melodrama is healing.

    I even heard of guys being asked to leave because of homosexual activity. Although, to the testament of the treatment center it wasn't because of the disgust they had with the physical act of two men together, it was because, as a general rule, you should not get involved in any relationship with anyone outside your sober circle for at least a year. Especially not with some man you have just met, and who is giving himself a try at sobriety for the first time in his life just like you. The complexity, the inaccuracy of our emotional responses is too great to try and include another being. On this point I totally agree with conventional wisdom. On the other hand, if you are with someone before you find out you are an alcoholic…

    We all walk to the table and take the chairs from it and make a semi-circle beside it. We don't need the table in the middle of all of us, tainting my story. With me at the open end I feel like a clitoris. I am the sensitive area at the top in the middle.

I sit and look at all of these faces, these grown men pursed up ready to cry with me. I feel a little like laughing. Laughing at all of us, at the seriousness of what we are doing outside these walls and how much we must be loved by someone to be here trying to talk it all through. Laughing at how rough things have been up until this point and hoping that after all of this maybe I can go back out and live a somewhat normal life. I look at them and wonder if any of them have had the nightmares that I have had. Some of them are good looking, marginally professionally successful, family men, you know. Some of them look the part. Some of them have the shakes still or are missing parts of their front teeth from falling forward onto the corner of woodstove fireplaces. Some of them look annoyed at being here, to listen to me, to be anywhere in general. But most of them look open and ready to listen to another man who has felt the way they have and perhaps even hurt the same. Most of them look with a small, comforting smile urging me to know that no matter what I will tell them they will still care about me. Some of them look like the rage of fucking Satan and, I suspect, are going to pass their time here and pick up exactly where they left off. Some of them are going to get out and do far worse than anything they did to get here. No matter, whatever they do is really none of my business. I skip their sadness and find mine again, with its melancholy winter ready to drip off of my lips.

The day after your first step is, of course, your peer review, and one given is that you must do what is called a 'meal statement'. Traditionally, the group has put together a poem that includes some of your story, inspirational highlights. One guys started with, *I had my first drink when I was five.* Beautiful reminders. So by now, the guys all know that I want to be a writer, and they will think that I have done so well with my first step they don't really know where to start, and one guy says that I am a writer and *why don't you just do it.* So I tell them that I will put it together before our next meal and read it just for them before I read it to the entire facility. They say okay.

I write this, and over the next three days I must hit a glass at lunch and stand up and read it for everybody who is attending the treatment center:

> *I've walked the walk and spit good riddance*
> *I've laid in the mid-afternoon*

Bent to the corner on days that smell so good
Needles and alleys and beatings, I've rallied
Bottles and valleys and mountains too high to climb
My parents were gone and my sister forgotten
My monster was fed and sat in his den
I was so sad sick and dying and rotten
Until I gave in and met all these men

    I think that it is shit, they all say that it is acceptable, and I can see that some of them feel a little less talented. There was a guy who was designated to come up with the greatest stuff for the others' meal statements. From now until the time I leave I will not hear him try to do this again. This has plagued me in my life.

    It is weird that being good at something can bring you such pain. I have never been exceptional at sports, I have never been able to cook, I can't build a car or fix a house, I can't hold a job, but these things, I am the best at. At giving of myself, at articulating what we feel, at developing an ability to think extemporaneously about a range of subjects simultaneously and keep them organized. In school, I didn't learn historical facts, I chose to learn how to think.

    I have excelled in this beyond anything I would have imagined, and many, many times I have seen excitement drain from others who believe in their talents. This has been a huge source of sadness for me and at times has led to my drinking, but always has led to me holding things back. I can't stand to see someone, someone who has marginal talent that is recognized by others, only to have me make them look stupid. I hate it, so sorry for me. But it is important to recognize that even though drug addicts have an abnormal amount of self-hate, the reasons vary.

    I haven't spoken publicly or written for print, but the good thing about recovery is that these talents, these things that can hold me from going over, are rediscovered in treatment. For everyone. People who can play music, people who played professional sports, people who knit, are all people that find the creative energy and mental discipline to do these things again. It is a rebirth. From the time I have walked in to rehab, any time I have ever been sober, I hear that I am gifted. I hear older people that have "been around the block" tell me that what they have heard from me is unique, distinct. It is new, and since I have been using since before I started writing I don't think I was prepared to have people look at me in such a good way.

An older guy from Chicago tells me he has never heard anything like me. I have been staring at him since I arrived. He is grizzly, and grumpy, and old, and probably the funniest fucking guy I have ever been around. One time, someone came in to a story of his halfway through and commented. Everyone sort of stopped, he missed part of the story. No one minded, even this guy, but he stopped and said, "Jesus Christ, _____, keeping you up to speed is like pushing a bolder up the side of a hill." I have respected his intelligence since I walked on the property, and he will stop an AA meeting to address me personally after I express doubt about how effective my writing or attitude may be. Through the charade of offices and doctors and therapists, I must have heard, "You have a lot to live for," a million times. But every time, it sounded sincere. These people just look at me with these broken faces, like, this time they are not just paying lip service. I feel it and appreciate it from them, and will always be thankful to rehab for this. I hear that I am good looking, that I am funny, that I am strong and beautiful and tough and cool and all the while I am waiting for someone to walk up behind me and accept this buffet of compliments. But…I am always just standing there saying, "Thank you." I say it again, and begin telling these men my history.

It is strange to meet strangers, and to have them interested in parts of you. *Interested*, in what you mean and who you are.

8..

A week or a month, it doesn't matter. A month or a year or ten, it really doesn't matter. Twenty years after rehab, I don't think the alcohol will care.

One day I will wake up and think that it is like any other day. I will be on a binge, and in that way it wouldn't be unlike so many other days. I will wake up and open my eyes and feel like the night before I had swallowed a stop sign. I will sit up in my bed and instinctively look for where I took my shoes off the night before. I never know where I take my shoes off or leave my decency when I'm drinking and the sun goes down. Other than shoes I will actually be fully dressed, even with socks, knowing that in the morning I have something to do. I will arise slowly, my brain pumping bile. It is going to explode. I will put my shoes on and stand up, unfocused, and search and find my keys. Outside my apartment the day will smell good, smell like maybe it will be good to give up drinking, but probably not. Probably…the tug has begun and there is an anger in my heart already that needs to be guided. It needs to be displaced. I will get in my vehicle and not think much of it; it is not a very far trip. I will put the car in reverse and patiently pull backwards out of the parking spot, then put it in drive to pull through all of the other cars and out of the parking lot. My knees will be cement and my stomach a trampoline. I will pull on to the side road by my apartment and drive towards the biggest street closest to me and won't be thinking of anything strange, except that I hurt. I will turn on the main street and go less than a block, getting nervous and tasting velocity. Getting into the parking lot my eyes will water and my chest will freeze. I will go into the liquor store there more out of force of habit than anything, and maybe just to feel a little bit better.

I will come out of the store with portable poison and sit in my car for a while. I know this feeling and I know exactly where behavior like this can lead but I don't really know any other way. I will sit there for a time and then decide that I feel too ill. I will open the Sprite that I have purchased and then the Vodka and put one to my lips, then the other. The Vodka will send me reeling, I will almost throw up but it will warm my entire midsection when it hits my stomach. It will make me feel calm like I am in a womb again. It will sooth my distress and suddenly I will have a predictable, reliable relationship with the outside world. Even as it will numb my senses and totally impair my judgment.

I will pull out of the liquor store parking lot and head down the street towards my apartment, wondering if on this day I will be strong enough not to go find Cocaine. Not to smoke crack. Not to go off of the deep end. I will head down the road and turn left towards my building and I will be a little slower than I may have been. I won't even see it coming.

I won't see your child running after a basketball, or even going across the street to simply meet you on the other sidewalk. I will be tuning the radio to a different station or looking at my phone to review my maniacal text messages to or from the people that can still stand to love me. I will be going ten miles an hour over the speed limit and will focus on your child's image just as it gets in to the middle of the street, and it will be too late. My truck will strike it in the body mainly, but because of the force it will whip its head toward my bumper. It will be violent and you will see it all. I will stop as quickly as I can and get out, because I will be in too much shock to try to run or turn around and drive away. I will get out and run to your child and see blood shooting from different points in its head and body. Bones crushed and diagonal like algebra. The child's eyes will be rolling back and it will probably be shaking from internal trauma. It will turn red from a cerebral hematoma because of the breaking of a blood vessel upon impact. Your child will be wiggling and involuntarily trembling. You will panic and try not to pick it up, to cradle it and tell it that you love it one last time. I will stand there and even give it CPR or mouth to mouth, if necessary. As the police are called and the caller is told that they are on their way, I will tell you how sorry I am. I will tell you that he just ran out in front of me and that I really had no time to react. I will tell you that everything is going to be okay. The crowd will gather, it always does where there is a young person injured. It will look and gawk and wrap its arms around me trying to believe that it was an innocent mistake. The police will arrive.

It will hit me like a fucking ton of bricks. My breath smells like alcohol, and I am the sentence that Jeffrey Dahmer should have served.

Your Son or Daughter will be rushed to the hospital while paramedics try to locate the internal bleeding and ease its breathing. The medics will probably allow it artificial respiration to ease the

effort of the damaged brain. It will be ineffective and academic at this point. The rupture and leaking of blood has killed your child.
I will do this, and it will be an accident. I will not intentionally hurt your child or deliberately affect your life. I will tell you these things and a part of you will definitely want to believe it, accidents will happen. I will take your child from you and you will be totally alone. No matter how many people come into your life after this day you will always feel alone. You will drive to certain places not knowing exactly why you desire to be there, you will be looking effortlessly around your house for something small. Something you think that you may have misplaced, maybe your keys or a piece of candy that you were really looking forward to. You will do these things for the rest of your life without ever really acknowledging them or understanding what exactly you are missing.

You will wander through children's areas at department stores and be racked with pain, or you will catch yourself dreaming about upcoming high school dances, and then, you will remember that your child was killed. I would not have done this on purpose, but that will not ever, ever, make any bit of difference to you because you can't ever speak with your child again.

I am waiting. I am waiting on the street in your nearest downtown to beg you for change. I am hiding in the corners of our society. I am waiting outside of the liquor store at seven in the morning to take my first drink, just to get me okay for the first part of my day, and am getting ready to run over and kill your beloved child. I am the wrath of our molecular addictions and my beautiful mind is totally subservient. I am smoking crack in dilapidated houses nodding in and out of coherence, enjoying my high right now because I have some score and won't have to be looking for any for a while. I am in Brooklyn, St. Louis, Miami, Detroit, Seattle, Los Angeles, Dallas, Denver, anywhere there is a name. I am in the bathroom at your corporate job doing lines off the back of the black porcelain toilet. I am at your child's party offering drugs. I am your high school student looking for drugs.

I am your ugly cousin who has definitely become the black sheep. I am your sensitive uncle who seems to slur his words on too many occasions. I am the poor in neighborhoods gangs have taken over, because if you are of age and have any wish to get off of your block alive you must have protection. Or do something not to feel. I am the CEO exploiting my employees and offering them insurance that when it boils down to it will have insignificant coverage as compared to what will be needed when someone in your family gets really sick. I need that extra capital. I am the pro athlete lying to your face as I sign your autographs. I am the sophisticated thief who steals from old people who have too much trust to accuse me of taking their jewelry over months. I am a young man in the alleyway off of a main street who is going to jump out at you, point his gun at you, as you tell yourself that there is no way it will ever happen to you. I am every black man you've ever been afraid of.

I am your son. And because of a psychiatric separation from reality after years of substance abuse or an isolation of my sensitivity to my cultural responsibility I am waiting to take advantage of you. I am a product of our evolutionary biology and of an unsafe environment when I was young and I will more than likely take you with me. I am a drug addict. I am down your street beating my wife and I am at your college selling you weed and I am never, *ever,* going away. As long as there are dime-bag sensibilities and enough human desire I will always be a parasite on your society. I will always be polluting your air and deviating from historical acceptability. I will be in capitalistic society and communist culture and tyrannical sub-culture and poor economies in the third world for the entire span of human existence. You somehow know you need me so you know your life could always be worse. I will always be haunting this place.

I am down there right now waiting for you, at the edge of your community. I am in school waiting to discover what a real drug problem feels like. I am in rehab feigning good intentions, and am under the bridge admitting I have no desire to ever get clean. I am speeding down your street, slow from the sips. I am you, just worse.

I am behind you right now, pacing, and I am going to come up quickly behind you when you're not expecting it and I am going to cut your fucking throat and drink your blood.

9..

I am sleeping better now after my First Step. I am punctuating my sentences with excitement and feeling relieved of a thousand pounds of pressure. I can't specifically remember anything I went over during my speech but I know that it feels good. It feels like I have huffed enough to forget the tough. I have been here pushing two weeks and, despite my better judgment, I don't feel like I want to kill any staff members anymore. Or anyone else for that matter. There is one problem though. Next week will be Christmas, I will be spending Christmas and New Year's Eve in rehabilitation.

A rehab set in the mountains of my beautiful Colorado home, where time and friction pushed up and carved out these majestic canyons and tip-top summits. Set in a place where oxygen is thin, blood is cold, and everything away from the metal frenetic city block is welcoming to the renewable soul.

We have to be in the main building by seven fifteen for our morning reflection, where we visualize the day and immunize from the previous night, and I am finding that waking up and walking out of my cabin, I feel good. I am not entirely sure what it is but after I have told my story I feel strangely liberated from everything I have done. I am arriving a little early every morning to listen to people mingle before our reflection and laughing with some of the stories. My laugh isn't so pained anymore.

Pitifully, the first step I initially thought was regurgitation, has become the proverbial 'first step' towards whatever. It is so predictable, and the story goes on.

I sit down next to a believably named guy and ask him how he feels about being here on Christmas. I am conflicted. I would like to be at home with my family and friends, sharing food and watching big men dress up and hit each other. But if I were at home, I know, there would be a very small chance that I would be sober enough to recognize that Christmas was even coming.

He says, "Yeah dude, I haven't really had a Christmas lately anyway."

"Why is that?" I say.

"Well, my parents have been divorced since I was young and my Mom, who I love, lives in New York. I don't get to see her very often, so I live with my Dad and step-Mom and we haven't been getting along all that well."

"Why not?"

"She is just always in my fuckin' business, always asking about my life. She is always trying to find out where I'm going and who I'm going to be with. And my Dad...he is just never really around."

"Yeah they sound like a couple of pricks." What a third-world nightmare we make of so little.

He goes, "No, I know, but they really just treat me like I'm twelve years old still."

"In the future we may have to pretend like we really said all of this: Finding out that your child is an alcoholic and has a problem with Cocaine might do that," I say.

"Ha, ha."

"No really, you have lived with them for a while, no?"

"Yeah, a couple of years now."

I can imagine his step-Mom in his face, orbiting red, these people never give up. They always want answers to mundane, irrelevant questions. Questions they may even know the answer to already, or if are given it they are no less ignorant of anything than they were thirty seconds before they asked. Questions with existential undertones. Always with the where are you going? And who will be there? And, that is what you're going to wear? What will you believe in tonight? What it boils down to is that people, non-addicts, are sitting on the elephant in the fucking living room feeding it peanuts.

What they really want to ask, what they want to know, what I would like to answer is: "WHY ARE YOU AN ALCOHOLIC? AND HOW CAN I MAKE IT STOP?"

Of course it may be disappointing because my response would be: It is complicated, and, nothing.

The funny thing is that, after being with him for a couple of days, it doesn't sound to me like he has any real drug problem. His bottom, his rough and dynamic weekends were morning cocktails for me. His tardiness at work? I couldn't even fill out applications.

"Don't you think they are worried about you?"

"They are worried that what I do may make them look bad." I totally sympathize with this sentiment, this attitude is wildly common with alcoholics. It is also something that is true more often than counselors and therapists want to acknowledge.

"So what about Christmas then?"

"It's not about gifts. It is about authenticity. If we are nice to each other at all, if we talk at all, it is all totally fake."

I say to him, "Victorian?"

"Exactly. Everything is pretty and superficially perfect. But there isn't anything deep," He says.

I pile on my bullshit, "Three years ago on Christmas I had my friend drop me off at the only bar that was open downtown. I walked in, I was drunk already, and felt almost completely comfortable in a place I imagine flies telling their friends to avoid in the summer. I always feel more comfortable in mud, you know what I'm sayin'? It was horrible. There was a pool table in the center of the room and a wall length bar on the right. It was actually kind of crowded, but with people from a horror movie. A horror movie about skid row, and fuckin' missing teeth…and lost families.

I walked up to the bartender and I asked her if she would make me a Long Island Iced Tea, she had a sense of humor about it, and with a giggle she told me she had no idea how to go about it."

These were not sophisticated alcoholics, they were patrons who had no time for complicated drink ideas. "I had her fill up a pint glass, usually reserved for beer, with Cuervo. I am not sure how many of those I had but I vaguely remember talking to my girlfriend on the phone and asking her if she could please come pick me up. I don't remember being very nice about it.

I woke up on my Mom's couch."

"Does alcoholism run in your family?" He asks.

"Yes, alcohol runs my family."

"Heh, *In* your family?"

"No."

"So what happened?"

"Evidently, I was able to get my girlfriend within a couple blocks of the bar while I was on the phone with her and then she was forced to drive around to see if she could find me.

She pulled up in front of a store somewhere downtown to see a group of homeless people huddling together, looking at each other strangely and bending down to pet something. To pet away the last remains of a broken man. I will never know what part of me she recognized first, but I cannot imagine what it was like the moment she realized it was me.

I had stumbled out of the bar and went down the street. I walked far enough to lose both of my shoes and end up face down on a dirty sidewalk, in the gutter, sleeping like a coma. There were homeless people trying to wake me up and a rich looking man, walking his dog, trying to convince the homeless people to help him carry me to his apartment."

"That would have been fun, he probably would have been gentle."

I say, "Funny, I guess she pulled up and stopped, and told them she was looking for me. They helped get me in her car and then called her an angel.

My Mom's boyfriend had to *carry* me up to their apartment, like I was five years old, and put me on the couch, and put blankets on me. I binged on Cocaine and vodka the next three days."

As I tell him this, my bottom lip sticks out and hits the floor, my eyes swell like balloons and I want to cry until I am pure again.

Part of me wants to call my Mom and my girlfriend and tell them how sorry I am. Part of me doesn't ever want to relive this day again. Part of me laughs. We, us addicts and hopeless veterans, have to have a sense of humor about what we have done. All these things are so surreal and ridiculous we have to smile a little bit. Otherwise, it would be so cyclical a hurricane would be jealous.

This guy says, "I have never done anything like that before, but sometimes I feel like I want to. I feel that maybe something like that, on Christmas day, may send them some sort of message. Like somehow I am jealous of that part of you, like doing something crazy might make people more aware that I have a problem," he says.

"If you are looking to convince them of something, the way you feel sometimes, the way you want to choke, you should maybe just give up. There is no way you can convince someone of something that they are unwilling to, or incapable of, believing. From religion to the way something is going to taste when they eat it, they may not want to believe that you have this problem," but everyone notices when you no longer care.

"It would be nice though, you know? To have them feel what I have felt."

"You know, they can't, they are normal."

He laughs, "What the fuck is that anyway? Not drinking until you wake up with a stranger?"

"Normal people do that. Normalcy is the ability to reliably predict how much and when you are going to consume alcohol on a consistent ba-"

"You need to stop reading that shit," he says.

"Yeah," I say, "sometimes our families aren't who we wanted them to be."

"Being in here isn't so bad," he says to me, "they aren't worried and I'm not partying. I just only think of the good stuff of Christmas because I'm away from the bad. I could think of worse places to be. My family loves me, I know that."

I go, "Hey, even high school girls have fat on their ass."

"It is what it is."

I do wish I weren't here for Christmas but at least I'm here for Christmas. I could have done so many ugly things and possibly brought pain to those I love. On the most culturally significant days is always when I have been the biggest mess.

It is always when we all have the biggest mess. The pressure and repressed, dormant dissatisfaction bubble into your joints, and I always feel on edge. I know there are whole families having love, and I am left to scatter what is left of my life. There is so much sadness for me around holidays, somewhere in the fourth dimension in the spot that psychologists and doctors have failed to acknowledge, there is something unexplainable. There is something impulsive and deep and I know and I am not alone in saying that during these times, I must drink. Oh, and please get the fuck out of the way.

On New Year's Eve four of us guys and five girls will stay up, an exception for the curfew is made and we count down and pop plastic confetti. It is the best New Year's Eve I will have had in over ten years. Maybe ever, I have never had a consolidated experience with my family, because my parents were divorced when I was four and not too long after that I was more concerned with getting drunk than getting close. I always wanted a knitted, predictable, structured family, and barring that, somewhere down the line decided I would throw a ten-year temper tantrum. I guess.

My god, I have been doing this for ten years. One day I woke up and couldn't stop myself from drinking more, a decade later I am sitting somewhere with other people who hate themselves like I do and subjecting my patterned failures to analysis. It was that simple. It doesn't matter when the ugliest part began, because people I know may be surprised to hear me quote 'ten years,' but I know that even at eighteen, I loved being fucked up, and never wanted it to stop. Then one day the party didn't end and my body felt different. I woke up and there was something drastically different about my hangover, it wasn't a hangover anymore, it was like taking a nap in the middle of a party and waking up to just drink more. It feels good to be here.

I tell this guy to try to have a Merry Christmas and wait to weep. As everyone wanders out of the main lodge at the end of the day I get ready to go to my cabin. I am here and that's all there is to it. My Father, against all better judgment, paid over ten thousand dollars to have me here. I asked him to do it, I was desperate for things to slow down inside me, and he said yes. I am never going to drink a drink again. I have never thought that, I have never said that. I have had New Year's Eves that I can't remember, and I have some I can remember, stealing Cocaine from my friend. I have had one where I wasn't drunk until 12:30am after kissing a goddess at midnight, and I have been there on one of those nights considering whether or not it would ever be practical to sell myself sexually to older men for money. I have had both, I have applauded it all.

10..

It is a year before going to rehab. I have a job, but I am barely holding on to it by a thread, missing days and showing up drunk. I feel like I am losing my mind. I have no emotional control and feel as though I am perpetually mad at something. I am always frustrated at niceties and hate going to work, even though by all available standards it is as good as any other place to work. I answer phones and read my books and try to push my boundaries on days that I can feel my arms. I am always discovering new theoretical standards that I have failed to satisfy in my life, reading about real tragedy and wondering if I will ever be in a position to do something useful to humanity.

Patience is a virtue and I conduct myself like a toddler. If I have to wait for something, anything, no matter how small, I get restless and tap my feet. I bounce around a lot and during binges I wail uncontrollably. Intellectually, I understand what I am looking for: Patience, tolerance, compassion, strength, wisdom, and courage, but am finding that free-base doesn't expedite any revelations. I am hunting for completion, to have more depth and always retain personal perspective. I am not sure what some of this requires but I know that what I am doing lately, on the weekends, with any free time, will not help me find any of these precious virtues.

Upon reading *The Autobiography of Malcolm X*, again, I feel compelled to quit drinking and using. I feel like I have been given a beacon, a light in the stormy depths. I spend any time fighting the urge or totally feeding it, to become something worse than what I am, but I feel in Brother Malcolm the purity and radiant nature of aggressive knowledge. Feeling something out there, calling and laughing, waiting for you. I read about him and from him and once again the revolutionary power within each of us boils inside me, seethes, exhausts, and becomes a nightmare week. I find hope, I protect and encourage it in these men I admire, and then, I'm me.

I consume the odd cocktail of history and frustration, and added to my physical fear, I have no chance at staying away from things that make me sick.

Dr. Martin Luther King Jr. said that a social movement that changes only people is merely a revolt; a movement that changes both people and institutions is a revolution. I wonder, in my troubled times, if I will find an institution.

One day, during this period, I am at work after missing the day before, a day where I smoked Cocaine all day. Cocaine is so fast, not in an exciting powerful way like it used to be, but with a nightmare of paranoid thoughts and racing laps. I pace constantly and always drink more to try to keep calm. Then, I over do it and am drunk and look for more drug to keep myself even.

I go into work and on my first break go and buy a pint so I can sip on it, slowly, all day, to keep myself calm from doing too much Coke the previous day. I go too far.

I slur my words on calls. People notice. I make too many trips to the bathroom and can barely keep my head up. On lunch I go to the parking lot and sleep in my car and puke next to my car and somehow head back in afterward feeling worse than I did before. My judgment is so off. I work with five other people in one big room, and although we all face away from each other as though we are protecting the computer in the center of the room, we have to constantly interact with each other and are never more than ten feet away from one another. I am way off, and take my bottle out of my pocket, twist off the cap, wish for a lightning strike, and under the front part of my desk put it into a cup that has some day old juice in it. There was over half of the pint left and I feel like I am screaming for someone, anyone, to take notice. It is incredibly stupid, but I am the bright shining sun that the universe revolves around.

Except that it doesn't. My co-workers are looking at me funny and I can feel their pity. But bless their hearts, they are too polite and shamed to accuse me of anything so ridiculous. This isn't the first time I have done this in such an obvious, distasteful way, but before I have been on a job site, alone in an incomplete room. Or behind the comfortable walls of a cubicle with protection. I must be sloppy now, to do something like this so out in the open, so like an alcoholic. This is a complete retardation of my sense of decency, my sense of what is normal for mature, capable adults. I am barely making it through the days at work.

I am crying hard at night even when I am sober. I mean hard. Not an audible heave or scream or anything that is overly dramatic. Not like I am trying to win an award, but like something is dying inside of me and bubbling out of my face. I am truly not attempting to draw any attention, which is not difficult because I live alone. But I am crying until I can't breathe, until my face is red and tears have soaked my lap. I thought that by this point, I hoped with everything I had, that this would go away. But it hasn't, it has only gotten worse.

There is no real temporal order to the way this dragged me down. It mirrors and reciprocates itself incrementally, and on larger scales. I have felt like it was going away, like it may have just been a dream, like it was just starting and was going to get monotonously worse, I have these feelings now and when it started and I imagine, I will feel it in whatever way it all ends. My symptoms and effects were at their worst when I first started, they are getting worse now, and will be worse tomorrow. I can't get a play on any of it if I can't theoretically measure its value, it is better than it was yesterday today, and will be better tomorrow, and I felt a lot better a long time ago. When I began, I had no idea.

I thought that at the least it would slow down by now and my body would feel better. I thought that at some point I would be able to handle situations that arise in our lives, the frustrating and innocuous, with grace and temperance. Instead I feel uncontrollably manic and monumentally sad at any insignificant disappointment or unexpected resulting emotion. I can't deal with regular, daily events, and their monotonous consequences.

Really, what it comes down to, regarding my addiction, is that part of me is still in complete disbelief. It hasn't registered, even after all this time, that I am this bad of an addict. I could think of a million things that I hoped I wouldn't be when I was young, many professions I didn't want to be a part of and many familial experiences I never wanted to repeat, this wasn't something I ever thought about. I never knew that there was a chance that my dependence on something other than food may dictate my life choices until the day that I die.

This is symmetrically polarizing, this is exactly how it would have to be. This is proportionately opposite of how I live my life when I am sober so it makes sense that I would be the worst addict I have ever known. I am now who adores alcohol, and who is a proponent of prohibition.

Being a drunk is a paradoxical divergence of two equal sides of my personality. I am comfortable with drag queens and military men, okay with effeminate homosexuals and gangsters, CEO's and homeless people. One day I am focusing on the expansion of my intellectual boundaries and the exploration of my philosophical depth, then I am looking for tin foil so I can free-base Cocaine. I am the definition of imperfection. I am reading about the Sophists and Plato and Aristotle and then I am wandering, too drunk to drink, mushing my brain.

This exemplifies what my experience has been since my conception and subsequent upraising.

I am rich and poor, beautiful and hideous and the weakest tough man in history. I *would* kill you, and save you and love you and hate you, I look good in a tux and feel right in a dumpster. I would die, in an instant, for concepts I believe in and I would run scared and hide under my bed when emotionally threatened. I am much more mature and secure than my age would suggest and I want to avoid any lasting responsibility. I want to marginalize my avoidance of personal acceptance and ownership of responsibility for all the wrong that I have done and I don't ever want to admit that any of it is true.

I have the most amazing, positive dynamic ideas and the most horrific and awful static thoughts.

I am religiously atheist.
I am cerebral and idiotic.
I am an inspired binger.
I am a roughneck prettyboy.

And…I come to after these tough weeks at work and drinking at my desk, putting in danger the one thing I think that can help me permanently stand up. My job. Losing time is like walking the dog, as if it is something that is necessary and you must set aside a certain amount of your energy for the process. What may be worse is not that you don't know what day it is or what you have done for the past month, it is that after long enough you start forgetting who you are and your anger and confusion can transcend any attempt you make at repressing them. You can forget what you wanted out of life or you can forget that once…you had hope.

Out of my mind and evidently alive I wrote short essays and read them when I became sober to learn more about the operation of my consciousness when I am using. I wrote this in the middle of a binge and have no recollection of its creation, in fact it really sounds like someone who understands intent and seems to experience purpose. I thought it was interesting to read, after smoking crack at two in the morning with people I had never met:

A NEW CONSCIOUSNESS

What has been ok to us, as Man, not just as men, is not so anymore. Or, it shouldn't be. As our present rapidly becomes our history we are forced to ask: What sort of legacy would we like to leave our children? A technological wasteland has become, it seems to me, the presumption of our immediate future. A world in which it is easier to talk with someone a thousand miles away than to cross the street and meet a new neighbor. A politically amoral vacuum, to my way of thinking, will become an imminent feature of American life for young people who may not be motivated to pursue radical change.

It may be time for an evolution in the consciousness of Man in the 21st century. A reassessment of the patterns of value he subscribes to. A new way of thinking about his philosophy, work, study, and expectation.

A new attitude toward work is necessary for our young people going into any work force. Especially if that work force is in any way a specialization of a technical field. Work should not be viewed as an emotionally irrelevant obligation; or simply as a way of providing a sustainable quality of life for ourselves. Work must be viewed as an extension of your innermost creative aspirations where you can see in yourself a reflection of society's needs.

A serious look at any and all study habits might be useful in understanding the stagnation of progression in some very intelligent minds. After, for most high school, but some, college, most adults in this country will live the rest of their lives without reading a new book, discovering a new wisdom, or learning a new trade. Communities as a whole must become, and remain, schools themselves. They must become schools not only intellectually, but morally, sociologically, economically, and politically. They must teach our young people to continue studying far beyond the incomplete education they receive at even our most advanced public schools.

The evolution of our consciousness in the 21st century has to start with our expectations. We have to globalize our thinking. What we expect for ourselves, for our families, for those closest to us, has to become what we expect for all human beings. Particularly in the contexts of justice and human rights. We have to fight for the rights of those we may have, in the past, misunderstood. Or worse yet, had a hand in making spiritually and intellectually illiterate. We must expedite the mobilization of our most precious natural resource: The minds and spirits of our youth.

With this will come new attitudes about topical subjects. The view that homosexuality is, and is only, a characteristic of biological functionality, will not be an opinion held only by the American intelligentsia. The understanding that poverty in America is, and has always been, about much more than continued exploitation of government assistance and drug abuse will be a view expressed by many more than those who are immediately personally affected.

What has been okay for us as a race must become something we assign to our history books; Nothing short of an intellectual and psychological revolution. It is time to stop focusing on the representations of our imperfections, or simply, the manifestations of our trivial differences, and time to embrace what it is in each of us that gives our time on this strange place some dignity. And please forgive me for this brief, inarticulate presentation of what I think are just a few of the relevant issues included in our struggles in the deliverance from all human suffering. Perhaps, after reading these words, you may be inspired to evaluate the evolution of your own consciousness. And maybe, just maybe, we can be proud again of the world we will one day leave for our children.

It doesn't mean anything to anyone besides me, but it sometimes is enough to read that I have subconscious dreams. Delusions of grandeur and exaggerated prose; the crack smoke keeps such writing short, and very immature. It sometimes is enough that I can be sensible and positive, not squeeze too tight. But sober, I don't know if I take anything like this more, or less seriously. Soberly, I don't know if I even deserve to believe in any of these fractured things. This is the endless journey of the eternally afflicted.

11..

'Visitation' is every weekend. Your family comes up, ready for the waterfall, and you can spend anywhere from a couple of hours to the entire weekend, gutted into soft sections, with all of the pain.

So I don't know how many people come, or why. But you should see these people when they visit. They are, every last one of them, there for a reason that the addict knows not. Their reasons vary and they are on their way and whether you have spoken to them at length about why they are coming or not, they are coming. Addicts haven't been comfortable with the unknown for some time. I hide and drink before I get to an exciting chapter. I also get to see this from the other side. I have been here around three weeks now and have seen many visitations and can tell you that each and every one of them has their own distinct personality and texture.

There are men, and possibly women, I imagine, who are realistically pessimistic about the arrival of their wives. Or their sons. Or their daughters. Or their brothers. Or their sisters. Or their uncles. Or their aunts. Or their nephews. Or their nieces. Or their Friends. Or their Mothers. Or their Fathers. Or their gods. We, in here, have been told, with the intent to help us understand its sociologically ambiguous origin, that our disease and drugs of choice do not discriminate.

These men in here have very contracted emotions as visitation arrives, they seem down in the dumps. I believe they in some way understand the hurt they have caused whomever they are to be reunited with. It could possibly be simply because they are embarrassed, it doesn't matter anyway I guess. The point is that for the first time in a long time depending on the frequency and longevity of their using they are actually showing humility. Or actual shame.

Rightly so. They should be a little apprehensive about seeing someone who has given so much and received so little. They should try to understand the metaphorical distance this person, or these people, have felt from them. They have felt cold, tired. They have tried everything they could think of to understand what they did wrong. They have asked themselves over and over what they could have changed. Or they maybe just started hating you and shut it out. They need a new beginning…or closure. Trust me, it happens both ways all of the time and this weekend is no different.

Some men are distraught and know that the visit will only bring the impossible details of property separation and parental delegation. They are nearly vacant of expression and are totally ready to leave. They are not here. They never arrived. And it is theoretically possible that the people that helped them to get here did so only to have them sober for the signing, so it is legally binding.

Some people are upbeat. Born of a curiosity that comes with infancy. That comes with the unknowing and transcendental ignorance of expecting something positive without really knowing why. They are here and they may have not remembered a lot of what they did, or maybe they have just not done that bad. Maybe they didn't steal from their loved ones and destroy them emotionally and financially. Maybe they didn't call everyone in their families and tell them they were going to commit suicide. Maybe they didn't binge and end up in strange places with strange people, and have their girlfriend looking for ways to be a lobbyist for prohibition. Maybe they are just light-hearted people and no matter what they have done are looking forward to talking to people who they have loved and affected in a very powerful way. Anyway, it is, they are here and walking around the treatment center and honestly making it feel comfortable. These people make everyone feel comfortable, they are smiling, they don't create tension and are not divisive in any way. It feels good to watch them.

Then there are people like me. People that make the rest of us sick. People who actually are in abundance at this, and, probably, every treatment center in the world. Others in rehab are happy for us, they are, but part of them hates us. People who seem, *more* loved, because of their addictions.

I have done unimaginable things. There has been, externally, when other people try to recapitulate when and where this all started, a slow, perpetually, progressive turn from me being a seemingly normal young man to the worst addict that they have ever been around. I used to be very funny, and still am I guess, but I didn't used to use humor to mask my discontent or for any kind of salvation. I used to be very quick, and still am I guess, but I never used to use it to withdraw from intimacy. I was a good soccer player, and still am, but I never used it to escape reality. I used to enjoy myself in ways that most people do. I took care of my responsibilities and had a good time in doing so, working hard and playing hard and generally living my life in a positive, natural, expansive way. I always had very good grades and was honest. Things came easily for me in a social way, nothing really seemed out of reach. Nothing. I had potential. I recognized when it was important for me to be courageous and when it would be helpful to employ more humility. There was a flow in my life that had to do with more than just aging, it was the breeze in the trees with all of the normalcy one could take.

Then everyone around me could see small changes. At some point my party lasted a little bit longer than anyone else's. I would still be up partying quietly when others were just waking up to get on with their usual weekend. I started wanting to drink at earlier and earlier times, which didn't seem so unusual because when you are young there are many occasions when your peers enjoy getting drunk in the afternoon. But at each and every event, I was the constant. The times got earlier and earlier than that as well, starting in the morning on occasions that didn't really make any outward sense. I periodically became unreliable. Things that were assumed about me suddenly became a little unclear. I was caught in lies that were unnecessary and trivial, and as such was never confronted because of their innocent nature. But I didn't used to do that. I became more unreliable over time, and then, began disappearing. I began crying a lot and was open about my struggles when most didn't know that things had gotten so bad.

Internally, I sensed a change overnight. I just held it together compartmentally, and never let one area coincide with the other so evidently that there was an obvious need for serious help. I was very good at this for very long. But inside, I knew.

Consequently, I have gone from a man who was proud to be who he was, just finding his way through life, to a man desperate and unsure of a life worth living. Socrates was right, the unexamined death is not worth dying. Wait, nevermind.

The phrase: "You can do anything you put your mind to," is said to young people universally. It is drastically and unfairly incomplete. It should read: "You can do anything that is within your capacity to do as long as you put your mind to it." I never heard either, the former may have been helpful. But the latter, the latter haunts me. I never knew that it would not be within my capacity or constitution to discontinue the practice that I basically institutionalized in my life. The process of self-destruction.

People like me, even dedicated to my drug of choice, still have an absolute, deep love for their family complete with trust and growth even after all that we have done, and the sentiment is consistently reciprocated. I have evidently not done enough to be written off. My lifestyle when I am sober is such that it gives people around me enough hope to not get tired of me and go running into the woods. I, against my better judgment, have treated people with decency and kindness enough to preclude me from the wrath of their anger when I have done something horrible. It has, just, been enough. I never set out to do things this way, I didn't want to live in polarity, but because of the shame and guilt I keep in my soul I believe I have worked extra hard at conveying to people that I care. I care for them, and their sad little stories. I care that they grow and are doing their best to avoid suffering just like everyone else. I have drunk enough and snorted enough and smoked enough to sicken the sickest and am still standing, trying to wear my heart on my sleeve. I think people in my life respect this and believe this has some honor, I believe that it is humiliating. And since that could be the genesis of humility as a character strength, it is useful. But all of my bullshit only confirms that I haven't had a say in my life for far too long.

I recognize my need to be outwardly decent, because of my shame in addiction and because that is the way to happiness in general, but altruism has nothing to do with it. I am just holding on to anything I can.

Nonetheless, it seems to have worked. I have shown enough people enough of my soul so that I am not going to be alone, a condition that sadly I do not share with the lonely and grotesque souls in rehab who have no one to hold on to, and no one to bother.

My family still loves me, deeply. I can tell they care, I can tell that some of what they experience in this life will be directly tied to my state of being. I feel undeserving most of the time. They treat me with kindness and sometimes with honesty, but mostly, I can feel their fear. They don't want to say the wrong thing, they don't want to endanger my sobriety by telling me what I already know. They don't want to collapse me in on myself by telling me what they have seen out of me and what they can possibly see coming. Bless their hearts, they don't want to call me a fuck-up, or tell me that I have caused them more pain than anything in their lives. Not all of the addicts in treatment are so lucky. Some family members seem to make a living off of saying these cruel, true, things to the addicts in their lives. Not mine. They still encourage me and support me and are genuinely there for me when I am down. I know not why I deserve this nurturing disposition but I am incredibly thankful for it. That doesn't mean that the people in my life are whom I would ultimately desire them to be, but neither am I, and they don't make me feel bad about it.

In fact, they all have glaring flaws. My Father, my sister, my Mother. They all have things about them, intellectually, emotionally, spiritually, that I believe are too incomplete to assist them in experiencing deliverance, that make me sad and hope for a better human being in the future. But I love them for it, and appreciate the drawbacks we all have to face. I love them all so much that it has kept me sick, it has kept me in my cyclical pattern of shame and disappointment for far too long. I can't imagine what they must think of me, but they are still here. They still congratulate me for being nice and hold back tears when I tell them I'm done. For some reason, they still believe I have something to offer. Some people here, poor poor people, people here on a handout, people here who have just been given some gift, have no one coming and no one waiting for them to get out.

The rest come, shepherded by the call that beckons us to our loved ones and makes us try and help. They are all here for all of us and whether we like it or not we have things to make up for.

They can visit any weekend, but the last weekend we are in rehab they are invited to participate in "Family Weekend." The families show up on Thursday afternoon to greet the dead. The loving hugs and warm embraces speak to the safety and consistency of the present environment, they know there is no real danger here. Not here. Everywhere else on the planet, but not here. They spend the afternoon with us and all is great, one family member per addict has an all expenses paid trip complete with meals and all the baggage needed for an impending family break-up. They stay in their own cabins on the property, on the female side typically, away from the dorm-cabins of the men. They are not allowed to set foot in our cabins, and rightfully so. Who knows in what way we could find to take advantage of them up here, I am sure it would involve begging.

On Friday they adapt their schedules to ours, meeting in the morning for breakfast and waiting for our lecture to pass by. They get their first taste of what this will be like when they are ushered into a building a short walk away to meet with the family counselor. Now, I am not sure exactly what they go over in those first hours, but I do know that they familiarize the family members and friends with the 'disease concept.' All that shit about us being sick, about us having a retardation in our neurological functioning, a bio-chemical addiction where our bodies do not crave food but alcohol or drugs, and typically a psychological addiction stemming from any number of events in youth. Though some people, some of the broken and mangled, had very well adjusted, happy childhoods. With no real psychological explanations, they ended up like me anyway.

    We continue with our meetings and our laughter and hope they don't hate us when they return. My Dad and his girlfriend have come up the previous weekend. They were only here on a Saturday, long enough to eat and see what I am doing. They brought me gifts on Christmas day, as if I have done anything to deserve them. This is my gift, a new start. My Dad doesn't need to be here for all of this. For this family weekend that lasts an eternity. Despite everything that has happened between us, the unhappy childhood, the rebellious attitude in late adolescence, not talking for a period of nearly two years, arguments, blame, we have come to a sense of real peace in our relationship. I have forgiven him for not being very nice to me when I was young, and he has forgiven me, almost right after each and every instance, for destroying myself. I am no longer mad, I don't harbor any hate or ill feelings towards him or my Mother, this is now my problem. And it has been for a while. So he just visits, and doesn't participate in the fun vacation weekend.

    Friday night, on family weekend, we have an activity that all of the family members participate in with the addicts. We are typically gathered in the lecture room and counted off into groups of six or seven. You could end up with anyone, any family member there for the sake of any other addict. It is interesting, each non-addict seems to care for you. They seem to identify with your pain, they listen. Not like in real life, not like when you are speaking to people about trivial happenstance, but when you speak of your addiction and the way you feel, these people *listen.* They have been through a lot, clearly, with someone they love and part of them just wants to know that what they have witnessed has been done by somebody else. They want commonalities in their experiences. They want to talk to God. So I pretend to be him. I tell them some of the worst stories, while we wait for meals, while we smile and pretend that we all didn't end up here, while we wait for activities to start. And I can sense relief in their hearts. They hear what I have done, what others have said, where we all have collectively been, and it eases the way they feel about the addict they know. Company loves misery.

On this Friday night, the last one I have, we have been instructed to put together a skit with other addicts and random non-alcoholics in about fifteen minutes. A skit that will entertain, and help us forget. My group writes a skit about Britney Spears. She visited our treatment center a couple of days ago and purchased property near the center, they don't want her here and I'm sure eventually she will decide to not check back into rehab at all. People do skits about rehab being shitty, we are assigned roles. There must be an addict, a doctor, a family member, a staff member. Everyone comes up with something marginally entertaining and then high school is over.

My first weekend here we were made to sit at a table and take turns being blindfolded with a large piece of paper in the middle of the table. The other members of our assigned groups told us how and where to draw shapes or objects that a counselor called out to the room. One week we held a 'values' auction. There were a list of values, money, fame, power, and some actual virtues. As each one was called out each group bid on what they believed to be important. I don't remember what we ended up with, maybe faith, but in the end, there were none of these awaiting any kind of winner.

These activities may be designed for a sense of normalcy, they may be designed to bring us out of complexity and back to simplicity, but we are told that they are to show us that having fun doesn't have to involve drinking or drugging. We are in elementary. They know it and we know it and I only believe that it has merit fifty percent of the time. We have not been told what to do for a while, and while some men need that, others do not.

The night winds up with our typical nightly meeting, in which the family members can attend. I say how cool it was to see everyone with their families, as secretly I imagine the interaction between these sets of people when they are on fire. When they are scared and screaming. And we listen to the family members speak about their experience tonight. Earlier, the family members were introduced by the alcoholic before we were split into groups. After I finish speaking in the nightly meeting, to my left, I hear: "Hi, my name is Mya, and I am here for Jay."

Mya. Mya Mya Mya. Over the last three years I can't believe what she has endured. She has been there and done that and been pushed into too many corners.

Mya and I went to high school together. She truly was one of the most beautiful girls in our high school even though she was two years behind me, and still is to this day one of the most beautiful women I have ever been around. I knew her best friend's older sister and if you know how it is being in high school, in the chicken coop, you would know that I mentioned to her how attracted I was to Mya. She rooted for me, most girls in my grade seemed to really think I was a sweet guy, I really wasn't. She gave me Mya's phone number and I called her. The most important social Moments of a high school career, outside of acquiring knowledge, are in pursuit of an attraction. An un-pursued attraction is one of the great tragedies in life, and we got along great. A short time after our long, initial phone conversation I was with some friends of mine, one of which lived in the same neighborhood as her and she and her friends met us all on a golf course in the development. We spent the whole night talking and kissing. It was special and innocent and didn't last past that night.

Unlike some relationships in high school, short term or long term, there was no negativity when neither of us called. There was never any rumor or anger, we simply did not pursue each other after that, I know not why, but I don't ever remember being around her again in high school. That was over ten years ago. Three years ago I had a soccer game and, smartly, after the game I went to a bar with my teammates. In walked Mya, and I remembered never forgetting. I was nervous and desperate to talk to her.

Mya is sweet, she is kind, she isn't like me. She is genuine and safe, she had a very good childhood complete with parental sobriety and support. It was not perfect, few are, but by all available standards, she was afforded infinite opportunities at personal success and professional development, and like a person with depth and maturity, she took advantage of those opportunities. A couple of months after I saw her at that bar I attended her college graduation.

At that bar Mya looked amazing, and I was getting drunk. I don't believe there could be anything more prescient about our relationship. We got to talking and she told me that she didn't want to go home drunk and that she was going to sleep in her car, I told her that was ridiculous and made her come to my house. I offered her my bed and said I would sleep on the couch downstairs. She told me that was ridiculous, we both slept in my bed and didn't even kiss. The next morning I had to go to my court-ordered alcohol class, my Dad took me because I didn't have a license, and dropped her off at her car afterwards. Those two had no idea how close they would become over the next three years.

Unfortunately for her, the dam didn't break until she was around.

In the morning on Saturday we all head to the building down the road, we accompany the family members and we have to be ready for the rapture. We are all assigned homework, it involves writing down regrets, resentments, appreciations. We are split into two groups because there are too many of us, here, and everywhere. We take out our sheets and each addict is forced to sit in the middle of the big group, in a chair, across from each family member who has come for the family experience. Then we are to read from our worksheets. It is impersonal, but when we are asked to elaborate on each of our points, that's when we get somewhere.

"Who wants to go first?" The counselor asks.

Mya knows before I volunteer that we will be going first. It is the way I operate, I want to set the standard. I want to confront the unconfrontable. I want attention. I want to be liberated. I talk about my regrets, my Christmas from years ago; spitting on Mya a couple of weeks before going to rehab, in the face, and in general, what I have become. My resentments focus on Mya's inability and unwillingness to tell her parents that I am an alcoholic, that I am a drug addict, that I have a childlike nightmare.

The major point of contention is that I am not ashamed of my addiction. I am terribly ashamed of what I have done and said inside my addiction and to perpetuate its existence. But I am not ashamed to be an addict, I think of it mostly as a unique medical condition, one in which those afflicted are luckier than anyone else on the planet who has a terminal disease: We can exercise a certain amount of choice. We can decide to what degree and for how long we remain so sick, and it is a beautiful thing to know that you are sick, but you don't always have to be.

When she refuses to tell her parents about me, it really isn't that big of a deal, but it creates a void. A separation. A situation in which she wants me to be relatively close to her family, but I can't because they don't know my story. They don't know me, and I don't blame them anymore after saying what I say. I am learning in here that I have made others sick as well, this hasn't been an exercise in futility just for me. I have drained people of all available hope and have made them worry like I worry about not being able to get more drugs.

She regrets not telling her parents about me, she resents me for my Christmas episode. This was three years ago, we haven't spoken about it since, and here, on this weekend, we come up with the same list. She hears for the first time how her not telling her parents makes me feel like I did when I was young, forgotten. Not worthy of mention. We share the entire list, except for my most recent regret: I spit in her face. It isn't on her list, but forever on any list, a grocery list, a week before rehab, grabbing her and pulling her close and spitting in her face will be on my list. The look she gave me could have prevented The Holocaust. It will be on any list I ever assemble that touches or not on the consistent breaking of previously unbreakable ethical and moral boundaries.

Every other regret or resentment or appreciation either of us maintains is reciprocated. It is a beautiful Moment at the beginning of a beautiful recovery. Her future boundaries include not being there for me while I am drinking, and not giving me any money any more. This is precarious, she really hasn't given me that much money but I understand why it is something she is unwilling to do ever again. She doesn't want to invest in a bad investment.

Saturday is racked with Moments of the nasty and heartfelt. Our Moment is unbelievable, watching other addicts and their loved ones go over what they have gone through is just as hard. To see these deep connections, these real people with these real loves just breaking in front of you is something that will make you want to remain sober. There is something about witnessing this externally, detached from its immediacy, that causes you to fully evaluate what you have done. This is a day that can be seen as the biggest step in a lifelong search for catharsis. In my opinion, it is the most important day I will have in rehab. I have so much to apologize for.

The end is welcome though, it is exhausting to go through this. When we leave the building and go back to the lodge I am ready for a drink. I make some tea and relax on the couch and think about 'Graduation' that will be held later.

Graduation is held every Saturday night. After dinner the alcoholics go to the dining room to listen to a guest speaker, typically someone who also attended this rehab facility. This isn't always the case, the only real stipulation for speaking to us is that you have to have one year of sobriety. Needless to say, of the people who leave this place, not many are available to speak. The al-anons, a term used for the support group for family members and people affected by the addict, go to their own meeting where they share their Moments and last-chance stories. After our speaker and the meeting our loved ones attend we are all gathered into the dining room. At the far end of the room a podium is set up with a microphone and the ceremony begins.

Clapping rings through the room at preset intervals, and the irony and sarcasm is lost on almost everyone. People think this will actually be the end.

Peggy, a decent technician at the recovery center is the emcee. She peppers the night with jokes off of the Internet related to addiction, the joy in the room is palpable if not misguided. This place is a sure bet, it is safe. She has a list of all of the men and women who will be leaving in the next week and these are 'the graduates.' The women are announced first saving the men to wrap up the evening, this is alternated from week to week. I am glad at my graduation the men go last. At the risk of sounding totally sexist, although I believe women attending from the outside would agree, the men are far more articulate and have a better sense of humor. I am sorry, that is just the way it is, we are more entertaining as drunks because of our chauvinism.

This lady that I have named Peggy calls out a name. Each time an addict is getting ready to go up and speak, a name is called out they have designated. It is a friend or family member that they want to introduce them. This person gets up and usually cries, usually drips with pride for twenty-eight days of sobriety. Twenty-eight days. None of us can believe that this is what it has become, in an entire lifetime, our proudest Moments have boiled down to us looking for an insignificant four weeks of sobriety.

When my turn comes Peggy calls out "Joe," my Father's name. He walks up to the microphone and when he gets there forgets to say, "Hi, I am Joe and I am here for Jay." But no one says anything, everyone in the room understands. He wells up and I can tell that he is nervous and probably scared of what all of this means for the rest of my life. He says something to the effect that this has been a long haul, there have been a lot of difficulties. He is not the greatest of public speakers and ends his Moment quickly, on the way back to our table as I walk up, he hugs me. He has been doing this a lot lately, and now I am getting comfortable with it. When he started doing it, it made me resentful. I honestly don't remember him ever hugging me before all of this began. It could be that my negative psychosis is selective but I would think that I could remember, out of eighteen years of living at home, a single hug, but I don't. I don't remember him ever telling me he loved me without something catastrophic happening. I don't remember him ever telling me, without me asking him to do so, that he was proud of me. I don't ever remember doing anything with him that I really wanted to do. We went fishing; we worked on cars; he watched me play soccer; we went camping; we watched what he wanted to watch and did what he thought was fun and my sister and I tried to become comfortable with being ignored or scolded or made fun of. And now he hugs me whenever he gets the chance. It took some getting used to.

I get up to the microphone:

"Thanks Dad. And not just for that. My Dad has given me about eight jobs in the last couple of years and is going to give me one when I get out. To all my brothers in here, stay strong, we can do this. Mya, I wouldn't even be here if it wasn't for you. (She smiles a smile that breaks my heart.) Since I want to be a writer when I leave here I guess it is only fitting that I quote Shakespeare:

> 'Cowards die many deaths, the valiant die but once
> Of all the things that I have yet seen
> It seems to me most strange that men should fear
> Seeing that death, a necessary end
> Will come when it will come.'

I just learned recently that you don't have to fucking go looking for it." As quick as that I am totally healed and beautiful again.

I take this opportunity to cuss when we are not supposed to cuss. Although I agree with much of the substance of the programs here, I want everyone to know, especially the overbearing counselors that I am an adult and I will do what I want. There is, and may always be, a very immature part of my personality that dictates that if you deliberately try and make me feel stupid or minimize how I express myself, then I will bitterly respond. I know it sounds small, but I am sick of being the bigger person, seeing the bigger picture, and being the bigger mess. We are insignificant compared to the expanse of the universe and one day it will be as if we never even existed, and this is your focus. I do not want to get into philology or etymology, but I can tell you that the way in which we use our words, our inflection and pace, our texture and tone and direction, are as important as the words we use. It should never be just about a singular word. If you don't like my attitude, you can go fuck yourself.

After you are introduced and before you speak at the podium you make your way to a table behind the microphone where there is a lit candle in the middle, and a candle for each graduate of the night surrounding it. The one in the middle is the symbolic burning of your spiritual flame, or something, and you take one from the circle around it and put the wick to the flame and ignite your passion for your sobriety. After you speak, you give the counselor, Peggy, a hug and she gives you a gold coin. On the coin, on one side it says *The Name of The Center*, and beneath it, *High on Living.* And on the back it has the serenity prayer. If you hadn't heard it before you came hear, you will know it by the time you wake up after your first night. We say it at least ten times a day, like rote. Like saying something enough times makes it true. When lighting the candle my thoughts race to the speed of light, my lips tingle and my eyes go numb. I wish I had days to explain; but get to the microphone, and I can't stand all those stupid faces waiting to waste my genius. I quote Shakespeare, think of Christ, curse, and pace back to my table with Mya.

  I am exhausted at the end of the day and Mya and I go our separate ways. She wanders to her guest cabin at the other end of the property and I go to my cabin. I miss being around her more and want to spend more time with her, but not at the price it may come with here. One guy got caught sneaking away to a bathroom with his girlfriend, he was allowed to stay but it was told to all of us at a meeting and he was chastised. There were several people who wanted him kicked out, wanted vengeance like elementary students. I personally was more focused on those who didn't have anyone to show up for them on family weekend. I wondered what would compel these tender souls to walk a straight line. Being a humanist, believing others are the reason we are here, to share and to love and to pain and to hurt, I can't imagine being absolutely alone, with no support. Greg has his cousin visit from Boulder, CO, he is a recovering Cocaine addict. But there is no need for his cousin to attend family weekend, and Greg's wife, as he sits and wonders, has told him that she is moving from Oklahoma to Texas while he is in rehab and sent him divorce papers. He wasn't very upset, but he loves his daughter. I think he imagines sometimes what would happen if she turned out to be an addict, what he can do to possibly prevent it, and how he will accomplish this when they both leave the state of his residence.

  There are many people who will not have the experience I have had with my girlfriend, here, on this glorious weekend. My other good friend here has no one, emotionally, and literally. His Mother went into a mental institution when he was young, his Father always wanted to be young himself, and the guy who ended up raising him was sexually confused. In that he was confused about whom to mess with first, my friend, or his twin brother.

There are so many stories like this. There are so many excuses for what we have turned out to be. There are abusive, psychotic, murderous childhoods, and there are stories like mine and Nick's. Through everything, we still have many people, especially our immediate families, who will do anything to relieve our pain. Evidently, it doesn't matter how or why you ended up without a conscience, you only have to worry about getting out of this. I can't believe how alone some of these people are, and can't help but wonder how in the world they have made it here, or simply this far. I feel sad for them, I will always have people who tell me I can do better. I won't imagine what it would be like to have people in your life who tell you this is all that you are capable of, and no one to rock you to sleep or touch your face.

The next day, Sunday, all of the family members must leave, after the most cathartic weekend of their entire lives. Mya and I are starting at zero, starting over, being babies again. I get up and wait the day out, watching people let go like their lives depended on it. For the first time, after dinner, when things are quiet, I think about the fact that I am leaving this week. I am going back to the place where I have inconsequential concerns, where my blood seems to boil with the discontent of a raging hostage: which is the world. Where people aren't very kind to each other and the only coping skill I have ever managed to develop is one of self-medication. It is a tall order even to visualize. I haven't done very well, without complete sobriety. In retrospect, I can clearly see, that every heart-breaking incident, every constabulary trouble, every ridiculous emotional outburst, has taken place because of my heinous relationship with drugs and alcohol.

I had dreams, you know. I didn't picture snorting heroin when I was young, I dreamed of owning a company. I never resigned myself to month-long binges, I always engaged in extemporaneous analysis and believed with the growth of my political inclination and leadership abilities I one day could make a positive contribution to the social scenery. I thought smoking crack was for crackheads and that for me there was freedom of expression, the liberation from racism of the human population, and the abolishment of global poverty. I never thought I would have trouble maintaining my basic decency and interacting with the loving fools who care about me.

I now, don't want to leave. I don't think that I am ready or that there has been enough time to heal. I think something I never think: I am scared. I am scared to fail. I am scared to succeed. I am scared of seeing things that are not there and of not living up to my potential. I am scared of having sex when I am sober, and of Friday night boredom. I am scared to go to bed tonight, and to wake up tomorrow. God forgive me for what I have done, I just hope people don't laugh at my efforts. I am scared.

12..

Two years before rehab Mya and I live with her best friend from college, near where I lived as a teenager. It is a nightmare, for her, her friend. Her friend owns the house we live in and has had to deal with so many fights, so much arguing. I have kicked holes in her walls and destroyed one of her doors. She has to live with someone who has become indifferent to physical confrontation. I don't understand that I am a boy, and these are girls. I am a drunk, and they are in the way. I cry to her all of the time, and she is too kind to show her annoyance. I get jobs and lose them, barely making it by. I now have my driver's license, so I can drive myself around, but I have a Breathalyzer in it so that it is impossible for me to drive my car drunk. I still find ways. My probation officer would have a heart attack with the amount of Cocaine I did while I was taking UA's for her. I was drinking a lot too, but I have crafted out a professional niche so that I should get paid to eek by.

We all lived in an apartment for a while, the three of us. Well the two and a half of us. They met each other in college and were very close through the entire experience. They are like sisters when I see them together the first week in the apartment, and after a year with me I will see them hating each other. At least that's what it looks like to me. Everything between them will heal but I will once again see the collateral damage.

People who are not even in your immediate circle are affected greatly, they affect the people in their lives who are close to them, and those people affect others who are close to them, and pretty soon everyone in the world is a little bit less happy because of you. Because, what I now believe, people do care.

This could actually be a good life. I do have a good structure, and I always have people peripherally, and Mya and our roommate try to make me feel as normal as possible. The house is nice, it is one side of a duplex, with a two car garage, three bedrooms upstairs, and a big deck in a nice back yard. It is in textbook, predictable movies for the suburbanite viewers, mirroring their medium incomes. It is in a good neighborhood and things feel okay sometimes, superficially. As always I am seething, and all that this stuff means is that I am a diseased, rotten salad with high-priced dressing. At least that is how I feel. But, like everywhere else, things could be worse.

Once though, during this period, I disappear and cross the line. In a rage, after Cocaine, Heroin, and bottles to feed the poor, I tell Mya that I will hunt her down and kill her. Although I don't think she ever took it seriously, in fact, I have a faint memory of her laughing at me like I was a joke, but it still was a benchmark Moment. I am at my sister's boyfriend's house, and I tell Mya something that is sociopathic. I have crossed some boundary, I would never have thought that I would utter words like these, but I have. I hit a wall in conversation-arguing and begin with the murderous threats, at the top of my lungs. And I can't take them back. During this binge, I have sort of become un-human. I end up in the hospital, after Mya comes down to Denver where I am and talks to me about still loving me. She is sweet and understanding, but I don't want to be alive anymore. I don't want to experience this body anymore without a sense of agency.

It is just more and more monotonous disbelief.

I don't want to sound cryptic, but again, I have dreams. I once dreamt that I would own my own very successful business, in an unidentified field. I imagined going in to work not quite thirty and behaving condescendingly, talking down to my secretary. What is even more sickening is that at the time, I think I was around nineteen, this did not strike me as disturbing. I pictured a world full of nice cars and crazy parties, of wondering whether cold water came out when you turned the left handle at a sink in Europe, and going to find out. I thought of having beautiful clothes and willing women. Sometimes I believed that one day I could be a professional skier, or a soccer player. I thought that loads of attention and positive praise would be a spiritually satisfying social completion. Thankfully, I outgrew this terrible dream. Others I did not.

As early as I could understand its significance, I wanted to be involved in an important social movement. I began my intellectual maturation a bit late, I was in my early twenties. But I always wanted to help change, even though I had no idea what needed to be changed. Then, I began reading a lot about Malcolm X. I started believing in revolution, and my materialistic fantasies gained strength and completely transformed into powerful feelings for equality. I don't know exactly when it happened, maybe in my late teens even, but I didn't know what was pure and what was fickle. I didn't know what potential our collective liberation held. But Malcolm X changed that. His autobiography inspired me to understand strength, intelligence, dignity, passion, and the absolute necessity to fight for what you believe in. Then, I read about Mahatma Gandhi. Although their philosophical disparity couldn't be greater, they actually do have much in common.

What was so great about Mya, even in this house with all of us dealing with me, was that expounding on this blossoming love I had for knowledge, when I was only just beginning, seemed to touch something in her. She could see that this may be a way out. And on one day that changed my existence, she introduced me to Che Guevara. So, with college kids across the world wearing him on their shirts and knowing nothing about him, I begin reading. I am reading more about Malcolm X, and two more books about Gandhi. I read about Dr. Martin Luther King Jr., and Mya changes my soul again when she tells me about Steve Biko. He was the Father of the Black Consciousness movement in South Africa, the most beautiful human being I have ever read about. The power and eloquence, the courage and sophistication, the harsh and human way Steve Biko treated everyone, people who loved him and people who killed him, is honestly something to create dogma around. I read *Mandela*, I read about Robert Sobukwe. I read more about the civil rights movement and about Mao Tse-Tung. I read *Narrative of the Life of Frederick Douglass*. I read about Belgian colonialism in Central Africa in the early twentieth century. I read *The Corner* two more times with better context, and I begin reading about theoretical physics with Hawking's *A Brief History of Time*. Later I read three biographies about Albert Einstein, and *The Fabric of the Cosmos* and *The Elegant Universe* by Brian Greene. *Origin of Species* is awesome. In that, I was awed. I read *The Brain That Changes Itself,* and then Jonah Lehrer's, *Proust Was a Neuroscientist*. I love neuroplasticity. I read my favorite authors: Hunter S. Thompson, Chuck Palanhiuk, Kurt Vonnegut, and thought of how amazing all of it is. I read more about Che, I am enthralled. I realize that the most important thing for growth is sacrifice. This means I believe in killing people. I read *The Assassination of Lumumba,* the most underrated, unknown, politically executed foreign leader of all time in my opinion. I read *Roots*.

And it all just sits arrested, frozen and suspended inside, bit by bit being forgotten with the destruction of my mind.

Why do I read? Why this insistence that it may save me? Their lives become mine. The textures and waves and eternal and momentous happened to them and because of them. If my life is a revolution, I am desperately revolutionary. These men and moments in history, these actual cultural and sociological upheavals happened at these men's doorsteps. And they all, opened the door.

If they can do it, I don't have to experience my own life. That was and is most of it; during the worst of it, I wasn't on a search for knowledge or enlightening wisdom, I was escaping in an entirely different way. All the while drinking, absolving myself of every threatening intrusion into my attitude or sets of ideas. I drank, and used, and tried, and failed while all of these people helped change the way I am actually experiencing my life at any given moment. I think I understand why such a pursuit would have made sense to me. But in its own selfish way, that also caused amounts of pain. I found things out that I didn't expect. If anyone knew what we have done as a country, not just the good, over the span of our history, people would understand that intentional murder and oppression of innocent people have been very bad habits of ours. The installation of repressive but friendly governments in unfriendly countries has been a big hobby.

For a country full of closet pacifists this is not going to sit well:

The killing of innocent people and of children is appalling. It is inexcusable, as far as innocent goes, and I don't believe any hero of mine ever did this. But the argument that people have made about Che is that his message was subservient to his brutality, and his record of volunteering for executions and giving similar orders after Fidel Castro's army took Havana is often quoted. He is reviled, and ex-patriot Cubans and bourgeoisie Americans compare him to Hitler. Adolf Hitler. My honest assessment, the people that were killed by him, the corrupt, rapist, exploitative, oppressive, men of the dictatorial regime, were sacrifices. If people in this country think that this is crazy, they need to read. They need to learn and listen and engage, and always remember how lucky they are to be in this country. They say he is an Argentine invader of Cuba, who stole power. Not realizing that the Revolution only won because of their volunteer Army and the support of rural Cubans. They may be more inclined to relate to the less violent Subcomandante Marcos, the Mexican revolutionary. But maybe not, because he believes in equal rights for homosexuals. One time he was being interviewed by a Mexican reporter, and she says: "What is it you wish to do?" And Marcos replies, "We are trying to change the world with fucking ideas." He recoils and contorts his face, "Excuse me, Miss, I am sorry for saying the word 'ideas'."

I don't believe in wanton violence, or the inevitability of war, or the necessity for murder in any personal situation. But when you read about social injustice, illiteracy, poverty, hunger, disease, racism, sexism, classism, oppression, the imposing of religion and using it as a tool for inculcation and obedience, and death, you yearn for someone strong enough to do the right thing. As horrific as all of it sounds, Che was that man for me. I have read all that he has written that has been made public, I have read four books about him, and especially, his biography by Jon Lee Anderson. Four times. I must believe in killing.

It was a change that was externally imperceptible, from my cushy Colorado suburb. But it was a shift in philosophy that shook me, and briefly had me engaged.

But none of this excuses the fact that I told my girlfriend, the one I love, that I wanted to kill her. Being a human being is strange, in that, no matter what we do or how hard we try, we will never know exactly what it is like to be someone else. What we can do is be inquisitive, and try to learn as much about people as we can, and base our judgments on qualified, informed reasoning. I wonder if I have done enough to warrant the benefit of the doubt when people hear that I have done things like this. All of my principle, and then pathetic drunken threats.

That is why it is so shameful to me that I have said these things to the one that I love. There is no revolution, and though she is not totally innocent, she does not deserve to be treated this way.

Soon after this incident I am in Denver, smoking crack all day. Trying again to remember to forget that I said this. It is a nice day, there is a breeze and it is sunny. I am fast inside from the coke but I feel like I am okay. My car still will not allow me to drive after drinking, so I don't drink while I am doing my drugs. When I get my car started after rushing the hits, I make a fucking b-line for the liquor store. I buy a pint and two 40oz Bud Light bottles. When I am exiting one major highway to get on another major highway I actually think I am in the clear. I open the first 40oz Bud Light and take a gigantic swig. If the Breathalyzer beeps I will just let it until I get home. While the bottle is tipped vertical, with its bottom straight in the air, my eyes meet the rearview mirror in time to see a police car race up behind me and flip on its lights.

I am going to prison. I got my second DUI years before this and part of my plea bargain was to not go to prison. I could have served the rest of my probation sentence from my first DUI in prison, or take a felony charge and get three more years of probation. I took the felony, and stayed out of prison. And I watch the cop and my heart falls in to my stomach, and as always always always, I am trying to bury my regret by getting high and end up creating completely new guilt. It is an existential tornado.

I began pulling over and as I slowed down in the emergency lane, he followed me. When I was just about stopped, all of the sudden, the cop floored it and sped around me. Again, I am thankful that somewhere, someone had the courage to kill someone else and require this officer to rush off to save lives, and leave my sentence with me. I never will actually know what made this cop rush off, but I am grateful. I wasn't near finished with my drinking and this would have put a serious damper on the continuity of my disease.

I was confused then and am now and will be forever, whether to use the past or present tense and not to confusingly alternate.

So I sobered up and read philosophy. I read *Zen and the Art of Motorcycle Maintenance* and *Lila* by Robert M. Pirsig. I read about Plato and Aristotle and Socrates, and I read more Bertrand Russell. I read *The God Delusion*; Richard Dawkins is an asshole I think, but that doesn't make him wrong. I read so much philosophy.

I read *A Million Little Pieces* by James Frey. Even if you think that he is a liar, he can write, and it is touching. I read *My Friend Leonard* by him too, and later I will read *Beautiful Boy* by David Sheff, *Tweak* by Nic Sheff, and *Dry* by Augusten Burroughs. I love David Rakoff. Normal people should also read these touching books by or about addicts and the people that love them.

I read about Mark Twain, William Shakespeare, Papa Hemingway. I read *A Heartbreaking Work of Staggering Genius,* and, *What is the What,* by Dave Eggers. They are both brilliant, and relevant. I consume the letters like an alphabet-addict. I read Chomsky. Dostoevsky, Tolstoy.

I try to read *Meinkampf,* it is possibly one of the worst books ever written. I read *Killing Pablo,* about Pablo Escobar. Even bad people can be interesting.

I try to read and interpret political science, philosophy, mathematics, astronomy, physical science, geography, race, history, criminology, morality, ethics, evolution, sexuality, philology, etymology, communism, capitalism, socialism, nationalism, naturalism, creationism, cosmology, and me. None if any of it makes me cry any less. Though I know more about why people cry in general. I am trying so desperately and failing so harshly at reconstituting myself.

You have to understand that when I am reading, or writing, where you see my body, where you see my eyes flash across the pages, is not where I am. I read like I drink, and I drink like a drunk. And one drawback to this eternal search is that my frame of reference is always on a sliding scale. I do feel like I am always living in my head. I am perpetually questioning the nature and substance of right and wrong. If someone isn't interested in reading history, does this make him a traitor? If someone doesn't give to the poor, does this make them counterrevolutionary? I don't know, but it is a study in anthropology.

So is this: Mya does make her own mistakes. At one point when I am in the middle of a withdrawal, I am sure I have a seizure, and am laying face down on the tile in the kitchen with my mouth bleeding, my teeth having smashed into the back of my lip and cut it. I wake up with her yelling at me, and I panic. If I have ever had a seizure, it may have been in my sleep. This time, as soon as I wake up I feel like I have never felt before. I am terrified and don't feel well. I don't feel like I am going through withdrawals, I feel like I haven't eaten or hydrated in a month. I feel like I can taste my blood, like metal. I sprint to give her a hug because I am so scared and she pushes me away. She pushes me and rages, and I know that I have turned the sweetest person into someone who is empty of compassion.

I will never know what I have put her through, but something in me tells me that this situation warrants a focused compassion. This is serious, and this is the problem: I have desensitized her to mortal threat. People go about their normal lives where their biggest problems are all very manageable, but I have spoken of death and scared her so many times that this probably isn't a big surprise, or as serious as I feel that it is. I have brought catastrophe around so much, it is too familiar. This is another beautiful aspect of drinking and crying wolf and swimming in self-pity. People don't know when you are real, you have been plastic for so long. In this terrible time of need, she has become unwilling to give. I won't forgive her, but I do understand. I think. She shouldn't have my forgiveness, because she should be in no need of it.

Something had drastically changed between Mya and I. It is here in our house with her friend. Something had gained Momentum, and it is dark and there is enough mistrust to appease McCarthy. I can't believe that the place we came from is gone and beaten, but it is.

It didn't used to be like this. There was a Moment, when I was crying at the beginning of our relationship that she took me in her arms and told me that no matter what we would figure all of this out and that there was nothing I could do to turn her away. Well, she is human. I honestly think that we have crossed that boundary and what innocence we had is all lost, there will only be disgust. I hope that I am wrong but know that I may be right.

Her and her friend have tolerated things like this for two years and really I don't know what sort of change I may be capable of. What is it that I have to look at to make myself understand that this will kill me? How much sadness can I handle before I decide that it is too much, that this life wasn't meant for me? I am running that thin line ragged. I know that I have stories. That thinking of Moments like these could be a full time job, that today or tomorrow or a year ago I could sit and write and fill a thousand pages of stories and nightmares and in ten years could sit down and write a thousand pages of different stories, and it would all read the same. I am sick, and sick of being sick. I can't even read any more, I don't deserve to know.

13..

I only have a couple days before getting out. In here they take you through step five, and you must continue, with your sponsor of your own choosing, when you get out. The highlighted steps here, and, I assume, everywhere, are steps one and five. Step one wasn't too bad. Actually, it felt like my diaphragm was filled with helium for years and years, and someone kicked me in the chest and ruptured some shifting balloon. Seething impurities out of my mouth. Step two reads like this:

2. We came to believe that a power greater than ourselves could restore us to sanity.

This touches on something that is very divisive in the AA community, and in life generally. This step is done on a Sunday in front of every man in rehab, it is supposed to be quick and direct. It is not done with only your group with the lights down. I am not sure why it was designed this way, but this step creates agnostics.

    This huge counselor, I mean huge, but is very kind, says 'go' to each person who is supposed to be doing their second steps and asks questions if he feels they are necessary. After a few guys go, typically Christian men, who have believed in the lord and savior Jesus Christ their whole lives and had him coincidentally ignore their pleas for years but now somehow they believe in him even more, I am told to "go":

    "Well, I don't believe in God, but I believe in people who do. Robert M. Pirsig came up with a concept, I believe that as man is the body of cells, society is the body of man, and ideas are the body of society. I think that what holds me together and makes me believe that I am insignificant is our collective ability as human beings to form new ideas. This pretext is how I turn my life ov-" he interrupts me.

    "You guys are making this too complicated. You don't have to be so deep you just have to tell us what your idea of a greater power is and how you handed your life over." His name is not Ralph, but good luck.

    "I don't know what you mean exactly," I say.

    He tells me to make it simple, I think okay. Okay! I remember him telling me that someone made the doorknob, in the room in which we have lectures, his higher power. I reflexively thought metaphorically.

"What, like he used it symbolically, like there was something outside, through a door, and he had to turn the knob to have access to it?"

Not Ralph said, "No, a literal doorknob. He didn't believe in God, and didn't want to talk about a higher power."

This guy makes us look bad. If, by us, I mean human beings collectively.

So evidently he is looking for something in between a spherical, metallic, tangible object, and abstract, powerful notions that are or are not a Christian God.

I say, "I believe that I am insignificant. That I am given very little time and what I do is going to be of marginal consequence. There has to be something bigger than me. This is my higher power."

"Good, moving on."

This whole time in rehab I am trying to relate it to my idealist preoccupations, and it just continues to read like an accidental lottery of ironic anecdotes.

Step three, which is supposed to be inoffensive and is really just a sociologically frustrating extension of step two, reads like this:

3. We made a decision to turn our will and our lives over to the care of God, as we understood him.

Both of these steps require a formulation of your theological opinion, whether you have someone pushy or passive asking. Even though the only difference between Christianity and Catholicism seems to be an accusation of molestation, you have to pick a side. Atheist, agnostic, Muslim, Jew, be somewhere. With men and women in meetings around the country, and everywhere, wherever AA is, you have people saying, "No, it has nothing to do with religion." No, my using has nothing to do with the high.

That 'as we understood him' is supposed to allow the way for any religious person or atheist, but what it does is put distance between people. Automatically there is, and there isn't supposed to be, but it is an imperfect world, a separation of what fundamentally constitutes the make up of two people who are supposed to reflexively respect each other. But there really is no other way, if you created dogmatic concepts and made the AA community commit to a Christian God, everyone else would be shut out. And it would be worse if it was the other way; there would be 'religious infringement' protests around the country, around the world. So the most amicable, ambiguous, compromise was made. A god 'as we understood him' was introduced and Allah laughed.

How does one turn his life over to God? Some of the men absolutely believe that it is about the literal transition from a casual observer of Catholicism or Christianity to a devout believer of the word of our lord, Jesus Christ. In the company of priests, praying incessantly, going to church, and wearing a rosary. Going door to door is probably not out of the question. An addiction to substance replaced with an addiction to religion.

I knew this guy in AA who came to believe that turning his life over to God meant that he was to make, ostensibly, absolutely no decisions in his own life. Or at any time anywhere:

"I wake up, whenever. (He laughs.) I do whatever God tells me to do, it's not my choice. (Laughs.) I do some work around the house. (Laughs uproariously.) I usually take a nap around noon, and wake up at two. (I am not exaggerating, this dude laughed again, hard.) You know, whatever. I don't worry about it."

I want to fucking punch him. God is lazy as shit.

Some people think that turning your life over means making all of your decisions throughout the day, the logistical and innocuous ones, but none of them over any longer period of time. You have to choose to get out of bed, you have to choose to put one foot in front of the other, you have to choose to walk into the bathroom and close the door behind you, you have to choose to put your dick in your hand, you have to choose to release your pee, and you have to choose to flush the toilet. But during the week where you go and who you end up with will all be planned by those that love you, but you have to choose to accept these plans. You will be at meetings, or you will be at work, or you will be at home, or you will not be in my life. And you have to choose to exercise your humility enough to concede your will to these schedules.

You can choose to let other people in your life play God.

Some people, people more mature than myself, deal with life in step 3 as they would have had they never heard the steps. They recognize that life goes on. What you have to do is understand that you maintain the power to make intelligent decisions for your life, and that there are things that you can never control. They realize that it has always been this way. You do not exercise total choice over most of the things in your life, now you just have knowledge of it. It doesn't mean you should try to control everything, it doesn't mean you should try to control nothing. You should try to change your attitude about the smallest things in life, find joy in doing chores. In going to work and being a good human being. Even if you feel no physical or biological feelings of happiness, force yourself to intellectually recognize how beautiful our small lives can be, and those feelings may just come. See that seeing is the rush.

Really, you need to do what you have to do, go to meetings if it makes you feel better. Don't if it doesn't. Respond to challenges with courage and decency and always accept responsibility for your mistakes. Atone for things when you have hurt. It is just like anything else, everything in moderation. If you believe in God, keep believing in God, just be careful about thinking that this belief will solve any problem. If you don't believe in God, don't manufacture it, but do find something that feeds your soul. Do simple things, and always, *always,* remember how horrible it is when you disappear.

Some people see that the giving over to God is only about the external, and they work on choosing the attitudes. In my experience, neither group, believers or non-believers, has had more success than the other. No group of step 3 interpretations seems to have massive success.

When I get out on Wednesday I can't say that I will continue to go to meetings, that I will commit myself externally or superficially, or that I will bend to any cause or means. I can't say that I will never drink again like I have before. I can tell you that if you tell me to take this seriously, I will laugh.

Non-alcoholics, people that love us, sometimes say that what they go through is worse because occasionally when we drug addicts use we get so fucked up that we get a break from what is actually going on. I can understand this perspective, but I want to tell them something: If the drug addict you know is a decent person, without the drugs, no matter what, if they are not sleeping, if they are using or not, there is never a break. There is never a time when we forget, or forgive ourselves.

I know how serious this is and if I am lighthearted at times or attempt to be funny it is because if I am audibly as serious as everything feels inside, I will jump off of a building. I will go, literally, insane. I will have a nervous breakdown. But I won't ever confuse this within myself. I have been close to death, I know this, so many times. I have barely made it, and I will remember this. No one considers my sobriety more importantly than I do, I am the one who will have to die, so allow me the space to decide and to cultivate what will be the best way to perpetuate it.

I will decide what all of this means to me. I will interpret, eventually.

This must be hard for people around me who have seen me battle so purely. I have fought and scratched and have fucked it up every time, every time. But there is nothing I can do; I have to figure out my own way, while using tools from rehab. I have to recognize and take action when I feel I am going to drink, but I will not live in A.A. Nothing against anyone who does, do what you have to do, but it won't do me any good.

Going through the steps now, I can't see it yet.

The day before you leave rehab you do step five. Step four, you should have completed on your own:

4. We made a searching and fearless moral inventory of ourselves.

I honestly do this everyday. Though I cannot say that it is fearless. I ask myself how I can become more patient, more tolerant, less temperamental, more wise, more knowledgeable, and then at the end of the day, I have to search for how I have failed in all of these areas. I sound like any drug addict: Grandiosity, self-pity, low self-esteem, self-hatred. But, as a disclaimer, it is true. This is a commonality between everyone here in this center, and more than likely, everyone who struggles with addiction.

It is not always an analytical operation. I do not think things over and decide that I am no good, that I am worthless. Whatever it is that speaks to normal people, average people, and tells them that they are okay and that they are worthy, and that they are going forward, is lacking in my extemporaneous experience. It is an inner compulsion, a fatal flaw in the chemistry of my neuroscience. Whatever I do I have to fight against this and tell you: Do not pity me. I am not a sad character and I have complex emotions. But I am a good man. The analysis is to get back to believing it.

5. We admitted to God, to ourselves, and to another human being the exact nature of our wrongs.

Father Rick does the majority of step fives. The preacher is 'another human being.' He comes a couple of days before you get out and smiles and tells you when your step five will begin. A day and time to beg for absolution. He leaves the time frame exponentially open-ended. He reiterates to you that it will last as long as it has to and until you feel good about it. His kindness is disarming. He is the tall white man with the graying hair and the glasses that is the grandfather of all of us in the white-washed high schools. At first the idea of speaking privately to a priest is laughable, and it makes me recoil when I think of why I should give this man my time. I am not afraid of sharing with a man of the cloth, in fact I welcome it. I have enjoyed being immature, and intellectually challenging religious observers, and absolutely have a distaste for conventional wisdom. That phrase, conventional wisdom, is the most descriptive term regarding religion in the history of the planet.

But Father Rick is a little different than a lot of religious men I have met. He is very good for a rehab facility where men only pray for their next eight ball. He welcomes differing opinions, he encourages sharing your doubts and ideas about religion, philosophy, the place of science in contemporary thought, and addiction. He smiles and meets your eyes when you speak and has a very slight squint, and he is *listening*. He has those eyes that smile with his mouth and look at you with the sincerest openness you can imagine. He is truly open, and not judgmental. You can tell he actively enjoys hearing the stories of these mangled souls. He says okay when you insult religion.

At one point, during a lecture, he asks if we believe in prayer. He singles me out and asks me what I believe. I tell him that prayer is "irrelevant and arbitrary." Immediately, I feel not as though I have slighted God, fuck him; but I feel as though I have attacked something this kind man believes in totally. I don't feel good, though he is gentle with this idea. He genuinely smiles, says "okay," and moves on.

He finds me now and tells me that tomorrow, the day before I leave, I will do my fifth step with him in his office.

As part of this process I have to sit and write down what we are to talk about, come up with things that I don't like to write.

We meet the next day, after a maze of hallways, in his office. A small, round, cubicle table is in the center of the tiny room. On our left are his L-desk and his little computer, and on our right is a wall. Behind the Frisbee-table is a shelf of books, some biblical, some not. Some are studies in God, some are studies of "God's Creations," none are imposing. His office as his cell works well enough. The acoustics are the same; the soft words ring back to you no matter how low you try to speak. If there were a God, he would be in this man's office.

Before I re-enter the confusion of society, I have to at least attempt catharsis.

We sit in his room, savior and damned, and I tell him all of mine secrets. They are mine, I haven't given them to anyone, and I tell him. I tell him of the time I took my father's car and took a check from him and wrote it out directly to the liquor store. For the first time.

I tell him I have, in the past, been unfaithful to the women in my life.

I tell him that I have masturbated to men, that I have stuck things in my ass for a better orgasm after being up for days.

I tell him I believe in free will, not determinism, and that my parents and the people they knew did some horrific things to me.

I tell him that I honestly desire a revolution, not in the physical or violent form, but that it is not just semantics with me.

I tell him a vague memory of stealing cocaine from my best friend.

I tell him that I have sat in a room, with a gun in my hand, with the steel in my mouth, on more than one occasion.

I tell him that when I was young, one time, my mother reached for a hug, and I withdrew. And that I have never forgotten her look.

I tell him that I stole cough syrup and pills from a girlfriend of mine and allowed her brother to take the blame.

I tell him that I once stole about five-hundred dollars from my job, and bought a lot of crack with it.

I tell him that after I did that, I genuinely wanted to kill myself. But that I came to rehab instead.

I tell him that I am always sad. Sad at something.

I tell him that I am angry, at life. That there should have been an option to come here for a short period, or skip it, and that I would have chosen, honestly, the latter.

I tell him I am looking for something, but I am so desperate because I know not what it is.

I tell him all sorts of things about the person I call me.

14..

There are some things that I think it would be good for you to know:

I am leaving all of this as a record in case the worst happens.

If you think that slavery has nothing to do with the conditions of our inner-city neighborhoods, you think wrong.

I cry often over how we treat our gay brothers and sisters in this country.

People should, generally, be nicer to each other.

Poor people don't constitute bad people.

Racism is a persistent disease in our beautiful world. It will eat us alive and kill our hopes and send the best men down the worst roads. If we want to have a chance at a better place, we need to recognize its existence and attack it with every possible medicine we can think of as human beings.

People who do not read books should not say to people who do, "You can't learn everything from reading books." It makes them sound stupid, even though they aren't.

"A man who stands for nothing will fall for anything." -Malcolm X

"[Einstein] argued that unrestrained capitalism produced great disparities of wealth, cycles of boom, and depression, and festering levels of unemployment. The system encouraged selfishness instead of cooperation, and acquiring wealth rather than serving others. People were educated for careers rather than for a love of work and creativity. And political parties became corrupted by political contributions from owners of great capital."
                                    -From *Einstein: His Life and Universe*

"I have learned many things about writing since I started living like this on the edge. Off the edge. Over the edge. On into the free fall of the monkey gang. Still, I know nothing about the technical stuff of writing or where to put a comma. What I know about writing goes beyond where to put your commas. What I know about writing has to do with where you put your heart."

-Nasdijj

I sometimes cry when I think of innocent people being held at Guantanamo Bay. Giving these men, even the bad ones, basic human rights, due process, and a day in court, are tenets of human dignity that is well within our capacity to afford to people. Jon Stewart said that principles are not principles if you forget them when it is hard, they are just habits. These principles do not just exist in the minds of the greatest thinkers in our history. People who disagree, should be held at Guantanamo Bay.

Honestly, Bill O'Reilly, Sean Hannity, Ann Coulter, George Bush? Honestly? These are the archetypes of the right? If there were a god do we think he would waste his own important time…

I mean no disrespect to the victims, the families of the victims, or the firemen or the policemen that were involved in 9/11, but still the most resounding, astonishing events of my lifetime were the murders of Tupac Shakur and Christopher Wallace. In that, they were two of the biggest stars on the planet, and not one person has ever been arrested for being involved in either murder. Not as profound or far reaching as 9/11, but astonishing. Terrorism does not surprise me, it has been and will be. But at the time, I thought that two men who pushed forward the American cultural dialectic at a crucial time in my life, were above the danger of assassination. I was sixteen when they died, and twenty-one for Osama Bin Laden, that is probably why I think this way.

And:

I used to listen to people to pick them apart. Now, I listen to help put them back together.

Please, don't ever equate the homosexual struggle for equality with The Civil Rights Movement. Ever.

I am not, anymore or ever again, afraid of death. My wicked struggles have helped me understand one thing: My body will die. My ideas will last forever. And so will yours, please be careful with them.

The most compelling and inspiring figures in art and society, to me any way, are those that are critically imperfect and profoundly troubled, but somehow are incredibly compassionate.

And:

I am drunk and high as I scribble these pointless tangents.

15..

After rehab my insides feel a little funny, they feel complete and dynamic. They feel as though they are interacting, and I feel strange.

My Father picks me up on a Wednesday, and we leave to go back to my area. Where my drugs are calling and my work is terrible, and there are liquor stores everywhere. I have thought about it a million times in rehab and there is no real solution. In the world, wherever I am, there will only be minutes between me and my downfall. Any time, any day, I can turn my car ninety degrees either way and I am off and gone and selling myself short until I die.

For some of the alcoholics I have met it is a gradual, progressive process. It starts one week with a six-pack, and a couple of days later a twelve pack. They told me endlessly that they could catch it. Then, on the weekend it starts a bit earlier than the neighbors. Then the next week it is a twelve pack each night and a stare from those that love, but their stares don't take you away like the beer. Then maybe hard alcohol and if you are an addict you find some drugs and a couple weeks later you begin missing work.

For me, it is immediate. I need to repeat it and believe it. If I have one beer, just one, I will be lost. I will lose my memory after just two beers, live in dense fog, and make new memories only days later. I will make excuses to get more that night and I will wake up and I will be at the liquor store before it opens and by the end of the day I will have exhausted all of my options to find Cocaine. I will eventually find some Cocaine and probably move to free base and maybe end up with heroin. EVERY SINGLE TIME. EVERY TIME I DRINK I WILL GET DRUNK AND I WILL TRY TO FIND DRUGS AND I MAY NOT STOP AND I MAY DIE. As kids you think that maybe you will see death coming. But when you are an addict, if you lose one battle, the war is always in the balance.

My Dad and I go to breakfast and he holds back tears the entire time. He tells me he doesn't know why this is so hard for him, but he believes. I am not so sure.

In the end, rehab was a place to start over, to be forgiven. A place where you can clean the slate and promise better things. Things also get more physically peaceful and consolidated. It is a good thing too, and here comes melodrama, I cannot take any more trauma in my life. I wonder if I gave it enough, if I cleared out the sadness enough and as I sit here and look at my Dad I think that maybe I have given enough, but the downside is, if I didn't, it will be a long fucking year.

We eat breakfast like two regular guys, and then we leave. It feels weird to see the breeze and to ride in a car, and to be able to smoke on your way to somewhere. I think of seeing people and going back to work and reading beautiful books. Then I think of being in my apartment alone, and not knowing what to do. With no one there to tell me that moving back there, alone, may not be the best thing either.

I moved out of Mya's house eight months before rehab, and it was the longest eight months of my life, really. I was up and down and out and back again every week. I would disappear for a week, and we hadn't even broken up, so she still managed to exert the energy to try and track me down. So many days of the same, and we all still want clean counters.

My Dad drives to his house where my car is and doesn't say much beyond breakfast. He has to go to work, and in this way he will always be old school. I know what to do, I know what I need, and ain't nothin' to it but to do it. So he leaves me with my car and I drive south towards my apartment. I think of all of what I imagined for my life while I was in rehab. I think of my revolution and the expansion of my humanity and working a lot, not missing days, showing up and having money in my bank account.

I think of buying a new car soon and of playing soccer more. I think of writing something longer than a paragraph, something interesting, cathartic, and of use to maybe more than just myself. I think of having children, of getting married, of loving completely with a full understanding of sacrifice, discipline, hard work, and I think I have years to go before any of this can seem remotely possible.

I drive to my apartment and stepping in it is wrenching. I remember crying here so much and saying things I never thought that I would say. I can't believe that I was here alone, with my bottles, for so long. I was so scared all the time, and so mad. I was a child, and still am. I take my bag into my bedroom and put its contents back where they all belong. I take a shower, in my own shower. I take it long, and hot. I cry.

I get out of the shower and move to my living room, get a blanket, and lie down on the couch to watch about eight hours of TV. There was no television in the treatment center, at all, and I have no idea what is going on in the world. I guess I could watch five straight days, or a month, but the news would still be the same. Unrest in the

Middle East, killing, starvation, oppression, Darfur, a child pornography ring in the South Pacific, the NFL playoffs, new celebrity babies. I read a book.

I talk to Mya on the phone and she is supportive and inquisitive. She asks me how I am feeling and is there anything she can do.

"Just...be ready, please."

She says, "I know babe. Whatever you need, I know you can do it."

The more you think that you have fooled people the more you realize that you were the one fooled by them. I thought that all of these people had lost hope, and swam in apathy, but they fooled me. They still have an extraordinary amount of love to offer me, and they never were fooled into believing that I was a bad man. I can't believe she would say something like this to me still, and I crack a wide smile, and get some sleep.

In the morning I go to work. The men at work know all about my struggle, even if they never have invested themselves in any way with me personally. I have always been open and honest with everyone about what I am doing, and these guys know the routine. I will be back because I am the boss' son, and I feel like quitting. Not because I am embarrassed but because when you are embarrassed you are forced to confront what you don't want to look at. My Dad owns a company, and now me. The sick thinking is imposing. I didn't ever want to take over my Father's business, but after rehab, I think that there are worse things in life than taking over a successful business. And I probably will never have the technical expertise or experiential capacity to take his job over, one of the other guys will have to do it. But I can make good money, and do a good job of my own. Maybe someday, says the alternating euphoria.

When I get back to work nobody that I work with asks how it was, how I feel, or what I had gone through. Not that it is a duty for them to ask but you would figure after knowing me for so long they would wonder what the hell I was thinking. But they don't, they have their own lives, and it makes me care about them a little bit more. I know they care, but they have tough times too. I have big problems right now.

After two days of work I have thirty days sober. I haven't gone thirty days sober, since the day I had my first drink when I was fourteen years old. I hadn't even tried, I hadn't even thought of it until my early twenties. It is one of the great ironies in life that you only find out that you are an alcoholic and that you won't be able to stop, when you begin trying to stop drinking alcohol. Before that, really, who cares? Everyone my age drank, almost everyone I ever met went out and got fucked up to have fun, that is what young people do.

So I show up for work and have changed my attitude. I want to learn and progress and be able to go to different job sites by myself and get enough done so that others in the company can come in and finish the job. I want to do well. It hasn't historically been this way; for years no matter what job I was at all I wanted to do was get through the day, get through the next couple of days, and wait for the explosion.

Things go about exactly as I thought they would. They are tough and I feel like and think about getting drunk a lot. When I am at work, I think of free-base when someone is cutting metal. On the weekends I try to consume myself with trivial activities and still I never feel the pure. I never wake up and think, *now this is the life I am supposed to be living.* I get up on days that are steady and still feel an inner compulsion. Something, my whole life, has been in the back of my mind telling me that I am not supposed to be happy. I have been an intellectual non-conformist and an emotionally unstable wreck and the combination of the two has not led to many good things. When people tell me what to do, or even suggest that what I have been doing has not been successful, I have to fight against my instincts. Because they tell me to do the opposite, I have to show this person that I am stronger and smarter than them, that they don't understand the strength of my will. Since, for the most part, people have been telling me things in my life that would lead to good, positive experiences, the opposite has not been fun. But, I proved my point: Don't ever tell me how to live.

I keep going, and revolution and ideas fade into sadness. For I don't think I have earned the right to think of how to help. And the worst part is, I feel like it may always be as such.

The only major criticism I have of rehab is that there needs to be much more interpersonal exchange with a professionally trained, qualified counselor. Peer-driven facilities are a conceptual solidity, but they are insufficient. Sometimes, it doesn't even feel like rehab, people criticize and are arrogant and have others to answer to. We need to know more about the deeply psychological and psychiatric causes and effects of being addicted.

Listen to my pathology, I have made a life of negativity. Everything in my mind and my soul tell me, don't do this. This is stupid and will only lead to pain. But my body, my poor psychology, reflexively want to shock. I don't really understand why, and probably I never will. Something inside me inherently tells me that a good life isn't for me. When things are good and perfect I feel uncomfortable. I feel out of my skin, like I am anxious all of the time. Like, there needs to be something wrong.

Returned to the monotonous, I don't really go and see my friends. One day, I am invited to somewhere with my buddy and I can't go. There were going to be people there drinking, and that doesn't bother me because I believe that people who can drink responsibly have every right to drink, and I never like to drink for the taste or the smell. But I don't see the appeal for me to be around people who are drunk if I am not, drunk people are stupid. I was. They do things that they wouldn't ever normally consider, they can be insulting or flirtatious when they don't mean it. I was. So I have to say no when I am invited to these places because I don't care to be around drunk people if I am not drunk, I never have; people aren't that smart or interesting anyway.

I try for routine.

Although things are tough, they are going pretty well. I find that rehab did teach me to take my time and recognize when I feel fast inside. When I go up and down and feel bipolar, acknowledge it and be mature. Understand what some small frustrating coincidence in regular life can mean. I cannot blow things out of proportion or lose perspective. I must remember where I came from.

My family has, historically, had so many problems with this I wonder if it is even in the cards for me to remain sober or together. I wonder not if I can do it, but if it is possible.

One time I went to get my sister, when she was drinking. A man answered the door, slobbering and happy, with a knife in his hand and his pants around his ankles. He shuffled around into the kitchen that was disgusting and I saw the empty bottles of vodka. I walked through the hallway into the living room and my sister was lying on a couch, she looked up. When she saw me I thought she became religious. I could see relief on her face and I told her to get up and get her stuff. The man wandered around but would only come so close to me. I stayed between him and my sister.

We got into the hallway to leave, where my Mom was, and we walked down to the elevator. My sister had bulging eyes, pupils like planets. Her hair was in a frizz and her clothes were dirty. The man walked down the hallway toward us and I pulled my Mom behind me, so I was between him and them. He stood there five feet from me, mumbling, stuttering, waving and stinking. I was going to demolish him if he tried to walk toward either of them; I was going to take out all of my pain and all of my disappointment in one Moment, and maybe kill him. A five year old could have beaten him up in his inebriation, and I was up to the task. He mumbled incoherently, turned around, and walked back to his apartment. Had I only known that I was ready to beat myself.

These stories riddle not only my life, but the lives of those that I love. They keep coming up, and even now I can't seem to get them out of my head.

The bitch of staying sober isn't in creating new patterns. It isn't changing my lifestyle, because when I am sober I only indulge in two things: Reading and writing. The hardest part of trying to stay sober is not constantly remembering specific things you have done. Not perpetually sustaining the crippling memories of your indecency. The hardest part is caring enough about yourself.

So you see, I am out. Inching my way back in to the free fall of the monkey gang.

Going back to work, driving my car, listening to music, looking for little hints at my revolution, it feels as though I have always done these things. Paying my bills may be easier with money in my account. These things are easy, it isn't the places or things I am worried about; it is the memories, it is seeing the people that littered the good days and bad, the emotional attachments I have to them, and the correspondences between these and those.

PART TWO

(YOUTH)

16..

Letter To The Preceding Generation:
We will only *ask* for so much longer. You are getting older and your ideas are dying. Homophobia, racism, xenophobia, detached from our own poor people, the idea that showing up to your job every day has something to do with wisdom, or intelligence, or morality - all these ideas will die with you. Do not push us, we are asking out of respect for you to step aside, and to stop bothering us with your uninformed traditions.

    I wrote this the first time I relapsed after rehab. I wrote it eighty-two days after I left the treatment center. I wrote it with an anger for the people I have met in my life, the people who are satisfied with stagnation. The people who are older than me; then I realized, I have no real frame of reference.

*   *   *

I have two memories, both cellular and concrete, from when my father and mother were together. I was around four years old when they were divorced, and I didn't speak to either of them about their marriage together until I was around eighteen. I didn't want to hear of my embryonic roots, I didn't care. My father built a house for the four of us, me little and trouble, my sister, my mother, and him. He built it with my uncles and his other friends in a very small town outside of Boulder, Colorado.
    The only vivid memory I have from that house is a fight. An argument, loud banging, distorted sounds, I could only guess at their meaning. I heard a slam, and I saw my Dad pick my Mother up and carry her out the front door, to the outside world unprotected, to the front porch, and drop her on it. I don't remember what my mother or father did after that, but I have retained that specific memory for over twenty years. I am still running from it. I remember being terrified and stuck, like I was being victimized in some way that I brought on. Beginnings are apt to be crude.

The second memory is when I drank a bottle of Nyquil. The budding seed of what was to come; liquid contentment. I remember the two of them arguing, yelling, and I remember, so short and innocent, coming around the corner of a counter. I remember seeing the bottle of Nyquil on the counter, and I remember picking it up and drinking over half of it. I am not sure why that bottle was there, if I was sick, if my sister had a cold, my alcoholic god ready to begin; and I clearly don't remember what my motivation was for drinking so much. Kids as kids, curious and devastatingly self-abusive. I do know that I drank it, and that later my mother told me that my father refused to take me to Boulder to go to a hospital, that she was 'losing it' because she feared me going into a coma. I survived, and the next memory is years later.

That was one of two times my mother insisted I go to a hospital to have it fall on deaf ears. The other was still in that same house, in the basement. My dad and some others were in the basement, playing guitar, changing the world, smoking the happy, and I was down playing with them. Central air did not exist in this town, local heat and wood stoves served as lifeguards. My dad threw my little football for me to go fetch and I went over and bent down to pick it up. I was not wearing a diaper and I flattened my tiny butt up against our wood fireplace. Searing pain and screaming for days.

Just like life, there is no point in these. I don't imagine that in another lifetime these anecdotal memories would mean anything, but they sound like the right beginning for a lifetime of voices and pain. It is only later that you find out that some children are raped by their parents, that some of them are locked in dog cages for days, the damage is done and the intellectualizing cannot quickly change the neural-riverbeds you have carved out for your own self-loathing. It just has to mean something that it is these memories only that I can recall about the start of my life.

When my Dad and Mom divorced, my mother moved down into the city, somewhere near Denver. My Dad got full custody at the divorce, and him and my sister and I moved to an older house in the town limits. The town was, and probably still is, called Gold Hill. It is an odd, juvenile, free-spirited mockery of a community. It may have been the place where the first discovery of gold was in this crazy rectangular state, or I may just be making that up. I cannot remember. The house my Dad built was a couple of miles away from the center of town, and the post-divorce one was right behind the only bar/restaurant in our community.

The town is dirt roads, a couple of stop signs, a school, a "General Store" like out of a lazy book, and then, just the houses. It still feels like a dream.

This is all going to hurt immensely, but it is the truth:

As the memories become more sequential and fluid, I am not sure what my father expected when he had kids, if he truly wanted us, but immediately before my conception he must have been vigorously looking for a maid service. I don't know if he desired a family, or if he cared, but I do know he shouldn't have had us.

My sister and I didn't exactly have chores, we had duties. Handed down by Chairman Mao. As I understand them, chores are rewarded with certain things. That is how life works, when you get older hopefully you understand that what parents are to do is prepare you for when you make your own life. Prepare you for the fact that when you do a lot of work, you will get good things, and that you better take care of them. I saw my friends being congratulated and rewarded when they worked hard or did something particularly responsible for their age. Because that is exactly how adulthood works, the preciously formative years we can never specifically recall are the structural groundwork for the development of positive responses inside of us. We did not get patted on the back. We did not get taken out for ice cream. We bought ice cream, we were afraid we would be taken out. We had a long list of things to do in the cold, perpendicular houses we called home. Actually...my father's houses we never called home when my sister and I were alone together. It was more like a formal, ruthless business environment.

Upon coming home from school, from the third grade until I left for college, we had to immediately begin for fear that he may come home and erupt before we had presented him with his masterpiece. I am not sure how he trained us for this, I do not remember being taught to do these things. I believe, one day, he just began calling me lazy for not always doing these things. These tasks. My sister and I would arrive at the house and immediately get the lemon-scented Lysol for wood and counter-top cleaning out of the cupboard. One time we thought of sponsoring our own infomercial, but I didn't quite understand capitalism yet. We would get a roll of paper towels from under the sink, and dust everything in the house. Knick-knacks, furniture, tables, record player, we might as well have had a log cabin.

We would try to be meticulous, try to get every corner, but he would always find something. I remember one time going overboard, cleaning everything I could get my eyes on because I could not take any more condescension. He came home and scolded me for over an hour for using too many paper towels. I now don't believe his intent was ever to hurt me or us intentionally, but intentions precede both actions and results. The results were those of self-hate, and no real self-confidence. They hurt. We would dust upstairs, the furniture in his bedroom, the bathrooms, the windows and sills, the glass, the doors, the undersides of tables. We would dust the banister on the stairs. I remember constantly thinking, obsessively and compulsively, I cannot wait to be older and let dust pile up to the ceiling in my house.

When he would talk to us about these things, such important matters as this, it seemed that he wasn't speaking to two beautiful, fragile parts of his life. It was very formal, detached, uncompromising, very angry, very demeaning. If my father was my model for God, he was the wrath of the Jewish one. His cold stare and his rough dirty hands were enough to send us reeling at any given moment. He would start by commandingly walking into his house, his purpose-driven life always on the go. We could see him scanning, picking, and we knew it was time. We watched out the window every single day for his car to come up the street, so we could hurry and find something to do to look busy.

After dusting we would move to the laundry. We would make sure to check his laundry basket twice, in case the first time we saw through his invisible clothes. We would put any loads in that needed to be done and finish any that had been started. And no doubt; he would probably be surprised to hear of it, but we shook through most of it. There was a tremble that acted as the voice of a longing to be left alone. If the clothes were dry we would fold them, and if they were his we would put them away in his closet or his dressers. If we did an entire load of his laundry, carefully and attentively, then put his folded clothes lazily back into their place, without matching the layout of each particular drawer or shelf, we were notified of the misplacement. Rome wasn't built in a day.

I remember one time, in that second house in our small town, my dad had a relatively new girlfriend. We had done something wrong with his laundry, I recall, and the first thing he did when he came home was told us: Watch out. He said that literally, verbatim. He walked through the front door, and nodded, while saying: "Watch out tonight."

That he wasn't in a good mood. I later tiptoed into the living room and asked him some question, and he turned quickly, aggressively, and frowned. He yelled, "Fuck you." He yelled with possession, and meaning. His girlfriend hit him in the leg because I guess she wasn't in the habit of cursing this way at a nine year old, and he giggled as he leaned in to her and said, "I told him I wasn't in a good mood." I never really liked doing his laundry after that. Anecdotal tales of fragility, I never knew how much hate they would help me to maintain.

After the laundry, especially if it was his, we would go upstairs and set up an ironing board with an iron. Later in youth we got hip, and moved the ironing board down in to the living room so we could watch TV while we did it. He would have said that, of course, we had found a way of doing it 'half-assed.' We would crisp his cotton work shirts, his button-up armor so he could go out and provide for and protect us. We would review each other's work, after each shirt the other ironed, pointing out its incongruity or fluctuating consistency. No, that sleeve looks better than the other; we need to find a way to spray the water on it more evenly.

We would iron and hang his shirts up, and never, ever, be thanked. Sadly, no cheering crowds or Nobel Prizes.

This doesn't mean that he was the worst father on the planet. Only, that we were either going to be great people with massive professional and personal accomplishments, or sad and lonely addicts still waiting to hear someone say good job.

One time I did a particularly large load of his work shirts, ironing and pressing each of his important dressings, and felt terribly good about him coming home. I was eleven. He came home and turned the channel to a home-building station to watch a man do some woodworking. He summed up the show by saying, "You wouldn't believe what I could do with those tools." I told him that I wanted this man's garage. My dad laughed angrily and said, "Ha. That man *works* for his stuff." I felt so lazy and hateful, and went upstairs to hang his shirts up.

After the laundry, the dishes. If there were any, which there never were, because they were done immediately upon the creation of the dirty dish.

Then, we would attend to the dog. We got one shortly before we moved out of the mountains and down to a suburban city that threaded along the membrane of the Denver Metro area.

We would take a brush to her, usually every other day, and we would walk her more than a mile away, circle a small lake in a clearing with her twice, every ... single ... day, and then return home to continue. In dedication to that beautiful animal, I would like to say that *she* always said thank you.

Next, would be vacuuming. There was a trick to vacuuming. If we could vacuum, have him fall asleep at some point in his chair after work, and we could walk on the very balls of our feet to go up to bed or to make dinner, we could preserve the carpet and its renewed structure. We could get away with doing it every other day. But we would vacuum thoroughly, for the most part, knowing that dozens of times he had come home and moved some of the furniture to find that we had done a real half-assed job. We swept and mopped the laminated areas of our mess hall and kitchen, shaking from the expectation of punishable failures.

To the credit of his vision, and his brilliant approach to parenting, to this day I cannot go long on a flat or dusty carpet. I count my steps, I have to have the same things in my pockets every day, I obsess about all kinds of tiny details, thanks to that carpet and those waxed-looking floors. Ten-hut. I guess I could think that it was his military attitude from his time in the service, but it goes well beyond that.

Yard work left undone really upset this man for some reason. Committing to mowing the grass, or weeding, or tending the garden, and leaving some of it unfinished was reddening. In the summer, after school and weekends were filled with that too. And it wasn't his violence that was repressive or dominating. It was his attitude and diction every day, regarding the nature and course of our lives. The unsophisticated and immature and childlike way we were unable to accomplish anything. It was his inflection, it was the way that I never remember him in youth, not once ever, deliberately making me feel smart or talented, kind or good.

At some point, we must make dinner, and we must make it non-repetitive, and appropriately complex. We must sift for recipes, and if we didn't, he would tell us that we didn't care for our family. He would tell us that he was working, and we were doing nothing for our family. We always had good grades, I especially, and spoke to him about school, about sports and girls, about leisure time and goals, not one time. Actually, for the grades, we spoke briefly at the end of the quarters, the semester break, and the end of the school year. When grades were coming home is when our schooling existed for him.

Because half of the time with those like him you are in hell. There are millions of childhoods out there far worse in their vulgarity and insanity, but there really is only one standard we should be measuring parenting against: Perfection. Since there is no such thing, I feel okay saying that mine was halfway to hell.

Because in a way, I knew then, what I know now, that I just wanted to know him. I just wanted him to tell me what was going on, I didn't believe he was an inherently mean person, but he never talked to us, ever. And he was always, always mean.

The hell was long and hot; I don't remember a minute without thinking of where he was in the house or of what kind of mood he may have steamed home in. I was sad and angry half of the time. I was always made fun of and never felt respected, enjoyed, admired, or blessed. I didn't feel like my life was mine, even at an early age I can recall feeling strange about being on this planet, but I had no one to ask. I saw other people with their families and thought they looked natural, I thought mine was natural in a more digressive way. Decaying, rotting, emotional carbon-dating.

Which led to the other half: Half of the time, I felt only pity for my father and mother. I have no doubt that this would be the first time either has ever heard of this, concretely, with depth. I intellectually saw these things from a different perspective than I did emotionally. They were two distinct, rigid areas of my me. They still are. Even as I saw and experienced some of these strange attitudes from others, I was detached from them. I, without reservation, thought these two people, my parents, were pathetic. Mostly my father, but my mother in a different way. I feel sorrow and regret now, but I mean it. They both seemed so isolated, and that they were coping with that through their actions with us. My dad was pissed, my mom was kind of lost. But at least she was very, very nice to us.

His garage was a dreadful place. A place to get vocally pushed around, to be forced to work on cars for extra money for the family. I would do odds and ends in the garage from time to time under the pretense that I would be rewarded in some way, at least encouraged. But it never happened. I would sand-blast car parts, buff paint, take apart engine blocks and set the parts in plastic bags, on the floor. I wouldn't say I was physically 'forced' to work in the garage, only humiliated into believing I wouldn't be worth anything if I didn't help support the family. A lot of times I believed that I could take physical abuse, if I didn't have to see the hate for me in his eyes when they squinted and he leaned in inches from my face.

I hate cars now. I would be in there all day, and at the afternoon turn I would get tired. I would see other kids running down the street, and I would glance out. He would smack my arm and raise his voice, "You working with me or you out there with them." I wish I would have learned more, then I wouldn't have to whine about it all twenty years later.

Any household projects, any side-jobs, any trips to work on the family friends' odd-job weirdo livelihoods, we were all there, and I was usually helping.

Schoolwork was the same, only I was the only one doing the work. From an early age, school was easy. The paper brought to me black ink spots of very solvable problems. Math, History, Science, English, the arts - even though I didn't become really interested in them until later in life, I think I understood their basic nature and the various reasons for their study. I was able to navigate through my classes with relative ease while getting into trouble constantly, for my running mouth. A problem from elementary, to the inspiring halls of junior high, to the sexually charged classrooms of high school. My mouth kept me the center of attention in all of my classes, it gained attention in some hilarious ways from all of my classmates, and cold resentful stares (and sometimes more) from my fluttered teachers. I could have gone anywhere probably, if I could have just kept quiet. But I couldn't.

I got A's so easily, and I don't remember a single time in my entire education that my father sat down with me and helped me with my homework. Not one time.

I cannot afford to believe that I was destined for the intensity of the addiction. I have to analyze for causes, otherwise I am left with just the effect, and too much I believe in my own goodness.

All of these things from youth. They seem so...isolating. They made me truly sad.

In late adolescence, I started understanding megalomania and self-medication. Licking my own wounds. These things begin so young. With no positive, external feedback, no reassurances that fill you with flowers, I looked for other things. When I was young I would hide and even read books, be by myself and get no looks. I would find new ways of escaping to get the healthy rush.

Then, as every addict at some point, I turned to the unknowable. I started playing soccer and produced the good biochemistry that way. Scoring goals and being cheered and never feeling so alive. Attention from young girls and making people laugh and finding favorite movies. I lost the connection with myself, my singular identity, and especially with my family. I lost an important connection that I know feeds into feeling that *my* family is now six billion strong. Not just me and my blood.

I would joke and lie, never fully understanding that I was looking for things that were simple. I was just looking to *feel,* good. Not be happy in a psychological or spiritual way, but to have that rush come up through that I felt not nearly often enough. Looking for the misguided interpretations of our minds, coming up with ways of giving our bodies what they need without being able to receive them from the ones that love us the most. And then, and if you can't see this coming you need to stop reading, as every other future addict on the planet, I found this synthetically. They call it 'experimentation with mind-altering substances.'

At the time I had no idea of its complexity, of its entanglement with my frustrated soul, but for the first time, I felt good. Even chemically, my body and my confused little brain, produced molecularly and electrically, the good feelings I believe I was supposed to receive by being looked at the way a child is supposed to be looked at.

I remember one time when I was 12. My father came home, I had a very big school project, big for me. I was lacking something crucial, we needed to build a house out of popsicle sticks. I had everything but the Popsicle sticks. I asked him if he could take me to Kmart and buy me some to do my homework. Ignorantly, since this was really the first time, at age 12, I had ever asked for help with homework, I had no reason to expect otherwise. He asked me why I hadn't started cooking dinner already. I told him that we were low on groceries and there was nothing I really recognized to get started with. He told me that I needed to be more creative than that. He went into the living room to give me some more time. I looked, I really looked, but shamefully didn't know any ingredients we had left.

He came back in the kitchen and I told him I was sorry, could we just go please. He was angry. I made a suggestion for food, I know not what, and he said that that kind of effort would get me only to the end of the block. We tussled and negotiated to see if I could get myself to the store, it never happened. He said that I was a baby because my face pursed up, he told me to go upstairs and get a long-sleeved shirt. He had me bring it down to the kitchen, with my sister in the other room, and make myself a diaper out of it. He sent me to bed wearing just that shirt, as a diaper, at twelve, because I could not cook my family dinner.

Of course, he came up hours later and woke me up. He said he couldn't let me go to bed without eating, he looked so concerned for me. I felt so horrible for making him do these things. He had me go down to the kitchen, sit at the table, in my diaper, and eat a peanut butter and jelly sandwich.

The next morning I thought it was over, the previous day usually was with him, but he told me to put my diaper on and go to school, and he left. I did not put it on, but brought it with me to school in case he got home before I did. I failed the assignment, but I think I got an A in the class.

My father still seems to believe that his parenting was more about making me think, questioning my intentions like that. But he didn't make me think, I did that on my own, what he did was create an environment where I never trusted my own judgment. Because, reflexively, my first answer has always been the most answers. The versions of truth that people get now are only due to the speed at which I can catalog any given number of answers, and find the one that will please them the most. Not please in a superficially gratifying way, please one in the sense that they will find me the most thoughtful and impressive. It is precocious when you are a youth. It is a horrible quality to have late into adulthood.

When something really broke between us, it was several years later. I owed him a bit of money, like one hundred dollars, nothing much. I was upset with him for the way he pressured me and I left the money on the counter at our house with a note that said: *Here is your money.* And then I went to play hockey with some of my friends. We had been playing for a while, I made a move, and out of the corner of my eye, I saw him standing, just on the outside of the hockey rink, arms crossed. Napoleon ready to conquer.

I skated over to him and he just said, "You better beat me to the car." And then he turned around and started walking. It was like he was walking from 1994 straight to 1965.

I skated over, grabbed my things, and went, just beating him to the car. I got in and he said, "I don't care what you say, we're fightin'."

"If that's what you want." I said cracking and defiant.

The rest of the ride was silence.

We got home, I took off my skates and he ushered me to the back yard. He walked me to the center of the yard, I could smell cocaine, even though I didn't know it. I had my Copernican revolution, I was Galileo. The universe did not revolve around me at all, it never did.

"Hit me." He said.

"No."

And he hit me. Hard. He had his hand open, not in a fist. But the hand was clinched as hard as it could be, it felt like a board.

"Hit me, tough guy." He said.

"No." I said.

And he hit me again.

"Hit me." He said.

"No."

And he hit me again.

"Hit me." Louder.

"No."

And he hit me again.

"Hit me."

"No."

And he hit me again. My blood was in all areas of my body. I was a good kid. I was horrified, pissed off, laughing at this pathetic man. Scared, what had I done...

"Hit me."

And he hit me really hard.

"No. And do you know why? Because I respect you too much."

"Ha. Respect? I'll show you respect." And he dragged me by my neck and my shirt back into the house. He dragged me to the kitchen where the money was sitting on the counter.

"Open your mouth." I hesitated, staring at him. He had me by the throat, he grabbed the money and slammed it to my lips, I tried keeping my mouth shut. He pushed the wad with his fingers over and over in between my lips until all of it was in my mouth, and yelled "Chew." Then he threw me by my shirt onto the floor in a corner with two doors meeting linoleum, the hard floor my most trusted friend, cracking my head.

After that I went outside, and sat with our dog. He came out an hour later and told me I was a coward, how pathetic, I couldn't even come talk to him after what I had done. I called my mother and left that night, the next day he said I was hiding behind her.

He had hit me before, but not like that. Not like a peer. He never beat me unconscious, never did anything outrageously violent, and he definitely didn't break my spirit. He broke what little emotional tie I had left to him. At a point when I needed him more than ever, and was just starting to realize my predisposition to depression and stimulants, he made me sad and alone for the final time. Something broke that night, something that I know will never be back. The physical strikes and the echo of my cheeks are secondary, you should have looked in his face. To this day, I have never seen a person as angry as he was. His lips were curled halfway past his teeth, he was as stiff as a cadaver, his neck and his head were still but his eyeballs were shaking back and forth. He was inches from my face, and now no matter what I do, somewhere inside me is a person who wants to smash his head in with a hammer. And it has been over a decade. I could not and cannot believe how upset he was about that, the man has problems.

Ironically, it was always the big things that he understood the best. When I was partially responsible for burning several acres of land near our town, the flames knocking at the front door of two different houses, he was completely understanding. When I got in trouble at school, or with my friends, he was always there. He brushed off the things that sent a lot of parents reeling, and kept calm in the face of situations that made most people panic.

When later I got in trouble with the law, he didn't act like it was cool, he just acted cool about it. From age five to eighteen, there was never a better person to tell about the big things that happened outside of our immediate family, that I was really scared of. Of course I didn't tell him everything, but when I told him of things I did not understand? He was gracious, and we got along like at no other time. It got twisted inside me, and no doubt has something to do with me now, but the only time I felt good was when things were really, momentarily, bad. Every other time, the days and weeks filled with the normal and untroubled moments of planning, I felt out of my skin. But not when disaster hit. I was cool, and focused.

Strangely, I do not ever remember asking him for anything, without getting it. I never asked to go on a trip, never asked him for money, never directly asked him for his help, to have him ignore me or tell me 'no.' I never had a curfew, he never implied that he didn't trust my adolescent judgment. And about major things, things that can send another parent over the moon, he would be as cool as ice. I never saw him lose complete control over himself and his emotions, unless it had to do with us, and that was when we were younger. I never saw this man challenge other people physically, or be disproportionately aggressive. When there were things that I thought were huge, that I was going to be in real trouble, he was very, very understanding, and handled those instances with a real sense of humor and perspective. The drinking, sexing, running through those necessary metaphors that a young male in modern America must, he never sweated me for any of it. He was a paradox, and psychically transferred so many good and bad things to me, that I don't know how to stop and stand still. I am trying, but I find a sense of balance nearly impossible. I have great character, and the bravery of an outnumbered soldier, but collapse and wallow over triviality nearly as often as I stand with courage. I was built to be a drug addict.

If your child, inexplicably, begins hitting you, then defend yourself. By all means, teach them a lesson. In no other circumstance would I defend that. Because if you have a good child, never, ever, hit them. Not in the face, or anywhere else. Not like they deserve it. In adulthood, the most the State does is confine you, and the arguments for the necessity of parental violence is a thousand years old. Hitting will never heal. No matter how hard I try, I cannot fight off the embarrassment and anger of the times he picked me up, or slammed me down, or hit me like a man, before I had become one. And if you do hit your child, do not be surprised when they look for other ways of making themselves feel good.

I could fill catalogues with clever little product lines, but with him, the gist is the gist and I am always selling the same thing. Let the healing suspend.

*   *   *

What I remember most about growing up, compartmentally, with my mother…is laughing. So much laughing. Learning the ability to laugh at something with your whole body, the kind of laughter that heals the world. And disappointment, cellular sadness.

I believe, with all sincerity, that in the fifteen years my mother lived alone and had us off and on, her and my sister and I must have lived in twenty-five different places. I had, with my father, stationary, consistent, weighted ugliness, and with my mother, traveling trips of stranger love and frequent fast food.

She had to hustle, she had to do what she could do. She grew up like my father, in the sixties. Big family, religious pretense, outside of Detroit, with an abusive father, and a mother who like so many others, accepted this or looked the other way. She went into the army at eighteen, received no real education to speak of, and met my father.

After they had us she stayed home to cook, clean, and wash us. To take care of us, and he went out to work to provide opportunities for us. Maybe nothing is more natural.

When they divorced, he got custody. He fought for it, and got his children.

She had nothing of experience, nothing to apply to the world. So she had to start from scratch, so we moved a lot, as she moved jobs.

I don't remember fits of irresponsibility, I didn't understand that. I didn't see someone too immature to be successful, I saw and experienced a transparent lifestyle, free of pretense and solidified recognition, I remember being free of the entrapments of sociological degradation. I remember being free to express my ideas and to be a child, to be young and American and liberated from starvation and humiliation. I wasn't emotionally castrated with her like I was anywhere else, I just was.

She made her mistakes, and in her own adult world she made a lot of them. We were always on the go, we were always having to meet new people and adapt to new scenery and become one with new environments. Had she kept us in a kettle, with pressure flying out of our ears, it could have been just as destructive as any other part of my youth. But it wasn't like that.

I am extremely good at meeting new people. At not being cynical, digressive, or a minimalist in any way. I met new people and was just open, just ready to explore my talents and hear new kinds of laughter. That is what it was, because of her grace.

One time she had been with a boyfriend, a boyfriend who I later found out dealt cocaine and wasn't exactly part of the senatorial debate committee; someone who didn't exactly take his commitment to society or to his community quite so seriously. But at different intervals, he seemed to make her smile.

They fought a lot, they made up a lot. He used to make fun of me too, or ignore me. He wasn't overtly mean, but he took me to a lot of places. He took me to his family functions and my sister and I were welcomed as part of that family, treated better even than the young people who shared the blood of this family.

One night in a terrible fight I remember hearing the blasting plasma of ringing eardrums that still constantly haunts me, the young lives of the constantly noisy. I was sleeping, in and out, and suddenly a bomb was coming up the stairs. I rolled over groggy, looking at the door. My mother burst in and ran up to the head board just above where I was laying. He walked in behind her, like a wrestler who had just been bounced off the ropes, centripetally swinging back with a steam of momentum. My mother grabbed me and I stood up, she put her back against the wall, she pulled me in front of her and pushed me towards him, and I stood there not knowing what was going on, or what to do.

This horrible human being, this terrible man, this drug-dealer who had no ethics, softly patted me, turned around, and went downstairs. I believe that this was the biggest mistake my mother ever made with me in physical proximity. Alternately, I think that she was too afraid to think and that she pushed her only son into harm's way to protect herself; and that she was just a young person with a young child, and knew that this man was irrational and high, that he maybe was going to hit her but that if he saw me or was close to me he would come to, and neither of us would be in any danger at all. Maybe that was the first time she told me that I was good. I never think of it, I have never thought of it until now. It was just a fight to me.

She always seemed to make strides to ensure the deliverance of my soul. When I say soul, I mean not some whimsical, multi-colored, gaseous, transmittance. But the soft and tender part of my me that I never let anybody near. The place that all of us hold dear to our hearts in fragility waiting for the right people to let blind with it. Even though she didn't articulate it, she didn't sit and explain that she was caring for my inner, she just looked at me in ways that no one else ever did. She gave me gifts. She could have said that she loved me more or that she was proud of me, for that she is wrong, but just like with my father, because of my unique, universal, personal gifts with people, just like with them, I always knew.

The translated powers of these small lessons do, really, resonate with me today. She may have been economically backwards, sociologically stagnant in ways, but to me she has always been the one person who I have had in no way to fear. No holding back. No miserable montage of egregious outbursts. Just a lot of laughing, and taking care of our souls.

As an aspiring adult, now, I can see what others said about her at moments. But as a youth, all I knew of her was happiness, was allowing myself to breathe, and that can never be a bad thing.

As I got older, grew into adolescence, and as a tainted, vengeful, teenager, I could talk to her. *Talk* to her. I absorbed the development of my kindnesses and compassionate idiosyncrasies because of her encouragement in me always, and they were allowed to progressively generate strengths from these positive experiences.

I remember when I was young, middle, and older, her just being there on the phone to laugh a little bit and tell me that 'that is what people do.' Not to be too hard on myself, to allow myself the room to make certain mistakes, as long as they were not permanently hurtful to others I had to acknowledge that no matter whether I liked it or not, they were part of the journey.

When I was young and got good grades she was there to tell me that I did a good job. She was there to reward me with small doses of the diplomatic candy that parents offer to their children for recognition. When I began playing soccer in adolescence, she smiled. She was excited and asked me questions. Thousands of rapacious questions about my feelings, excitements, new friends, and what I was to wear. In high school when I was starting to date she was there to laugh at my sexist jokes and throw me maternal dirty looks, knowing that inside I was capable of much deeper love for the opposite sex. When I got into trouble in school she was there to help me through it, to hide from my dad the unnecessary trouble of telling Dad of these trivial, impetuous, ultimately shaping moments in a young man's life.

When I went to Europe to play soccer in the two largest youth tournaments of the world, it was her I wish could have seen me, in all my glory, riding that bench.

She was there to encourage me to pursue acting, by way of modeling, when everyone else thought it was uproarious. She helped me pay for as much of it as she could and told me I was capable of anything.

She let me go to the places that it is so important for young people to go. To play in our minds and embrace our imaginations. When I was young, and in the safety of the intergalactic tribunal, I could be the policeman from outer space. I could be the righteous criminal only committing crimes in the city that I was trying to help, be Robin Hood. I could set up an entire book store in my room and have customers coming in and out all day trying to buy the books that I did not want to sell, I could negotiate with these people, being both voices without being called crazy or made to feel effeminate.

I could go down to the park.

I could bring my different uniforms. I would write down both of the line-ups from the NBA all-star game and log all of the stats from the game and act them out on the neighborhood basketball court.

I could do my homework and then play video games for hours. Not because I was lazy or irresponsible, not because I was already allowing my septic little self to be made of crap, but because I was young and I had to indulge.

I could set up all kinds of things with my sister and we could interact in a healthy way. Which we never did. We always fought.

When I was in junior high I could talk to her about things. We didn't always have the best lifestyle. We didn't ride in limousines too often. But I was free, free to be me.

When I was in high school she bought a house only a couple of blocks away from my father, and had to be closer to the clash between me and him. Which was always a battle for them both. But my mother is a female, he is not. I remember their insults at all of the meeting places in Boulder when we would make an exchange in my early life. I remember their fighting whenever anything more than something totally innocuous was going on with our lives. Any decision to be made was a hassle, and she really had no legal right to make any of those decisions, but she always fought. I remember her not always being there. I remember her always trying to be there.

It was her who I would always go to, to expose my soul. She was always supportive of who I was, even if my deeds were misleading. She was always ready to give condolences when I had lost a part of myself.

It was her who I would go to later, when I had done something unimaginable within my addiction, and she could see right through it. Even before she had her own battles, she could see that the catalyst for these nasty habits of treating people badly was simply because I had a nasty habit. She would tell me, not accept negotiation, that I was a good man and that there were ways for me to make up for it.

It has always been her to be there to nourish me back to health.

She is indirectly responsible for the budding feelings of social consciousness I would one day turn into an ideological compound of daily activity. She showed me, as my father did with his most obvious of deeds, the way she experienced the world. Then, later, I would realize how important her demeanor was. Because what I have become has more than likely been innate. A courageous, impotent fighter for the equal rights of everyone left behind. They would have been there anyway. I would probably have eventually read and wrote and believed in something, but her behavior activated these things far younger than I had ever noticed. Her simplicity, and her social style were always bent towards non-judgment. She thought people could be crazy, but not that the world was full of crazy people.

The building of a new nation begins with the woman. The woman is the first teacher of the child, the message she gives to that child, the child gives to the world. Malcolm X said that to me, and I can say that her message was clear, if subtle. Racism was always unthinkable and unobtainable for her. And it is for me. Shunning the poor or disconnecting ourselves from the poor was always unreachable for her, and it is for me. Global justice was something she believed in even if she didn't express it, and so do I.

I took these small seeds and cultivated them into a storm of revolutionary concepts, further than anyone ever would have imagined, even her. I have no outlet for it all, but that is the point. First this, then that. I will have my Communist Manifesto.

Because of what she showed me, what she gave me, what she allowed me to believe, I continued. She showed me that there just might be a heaven, she allowed me to believe that there are good people here, that, there are those who will love you just for what you are. They will not try to change you, not show you that you are not good enough, they will simply…accept you. That was the most important gift of my life.

In my total life, the proper name I carry with me that will eventually contain every thought and action I have ever experienced, she will be the only one who constantly sees the intelligence in the way I try to do every little thing. We will even use together, and others in my life will despise her for it. People will see things and say things, but there is nothing I can do about the fact that she will always look at me the way she does. Like she is happy she met me, like I am a blessing here, like her life is better for having known me and brought me here.

It helps to balance the insecurity with confidence, and move all the panic unto processed curiosity. Without her, I will not live to see thirty.

I have maintained hope throughout because of the small things that were offered to me in such human ways. By her, by both of my parents. In all of their hypocrisy and degeneration.

When I sit to scribble some 'Letter to the Preceding Generation', they are, and they are not, who I have in mind. Families are the gravity we all take for granted.

(IMAGINATION)
17..

It starts when I open my eyes. It pulsates and is uncomfortable; it actually feels like there are air pockets in my brain. I can feel that my brain is muscle and tissue, and it feels contorted.

This coincides with tingling in my hands and feet. Not excited, not tingling, but as appendages that have been forgotten by my circulatory system. They feel dry and light, they crisp and flake when I rub them together, dust-balls at the end of my arms and legs. My fingernails are cardboard, tinted yellow-brown, they are hard and crack when I look at them. I cry and curse at them because in this condition, I cannot write.

Dry isn't exactly the adjective. It isn't dry. My eyes feel like exit signs, buzzing in constancy. They feel so so wide, my pupils searching for any light to inform my malfunctioning brain of its environment. When I blink I see movies, violence, sexual deviance, rape, murder, playing themselves out on the backs of my eyelids in a matter of seconds. I can squint and try to focus to see deeper into the backs of them, but the images become more elusive. They reduce in focus and clarity the more I try to see them for what they are. Conscious hallucinations. I try not to blink, but I am brittle, and my eyes haven't closed in days.

The Withdrawal begins as a small pin pushing in the center of the top of my head. It waves and crests to the air pockets, bringing with it synaptic chaos and unbearable emotion. Emotion that chokes and forces tears and large, poorly timed smiles. It flows to my cracked, beaten eyeballs. It waves down to my chin through my mouth, acid comes up. My poor little taste buds, victims of napalm. My mouth feels so coarse, and my teeth don't taste like mine.

My teeth usually have a familiar texture, and my tongue runs smooth across their broken tops. But not today. The edges feel so sharp and I have to keep my jaw widened to let my tongue sit in its own space. Away from the fire. My tongue is destroyed, sandpaper surface. My gums are swollen, rocks sit jagged in the puffed up sponge. They hurt. My lips feel like I have been giving head for a month. I cannot even try eating. If I am able to chew, the food has no taste, and when I swallow it feels any second will bring esophageal varices. Blood and gushing, sending me screaming, and I have to breathe. Long slow breaths. The pain in my throat when I try to swallow is unbearable, just more drink please.

The waves get bigger and smaller, more profound and physically painful. It hurts, help me. I feel a liquid dripping into the back of my throat. I saw a story once and that must be it: Spinal fluid is dripping through my nasal passage, I know it. Spinal fluid is going down my throat and into my stomach and it will poison me and I am going to die. My thoughts are racing so fast and I feel like I have taken way too many hits of acid, but I haven't had any in years. Something is wrong, my brain must be bleeding. I pick up the phone, hit 'phone,' and put my thumb on the 9. Not yet, I can take this.

And my nose hurts, like I have been punched square in the bridge of it by someone trained to fight. It throbs and shoots and wells my eyes at different and unpredictable moments, and at times I think it has burst with blood dripping down onto my shirt and my god there is so much blood but I don't really want to look because if I do then I will have to call the hospital and if I call them then I know I will never have a drink again and I am so afraid that all of the blood will drain from my brain through my nose. I look. It is just mucus, the rejection of fluids from the tiny protectors of my body. They want it out.

But the wave is rolling around up in my brain, my mind. A misguided electrical current that brings a suitcase full of nausea and fear. It hits the back of my head and back to my eyes and to my ears sending piercing sirens, someone has a dog whistle. It comes rushing through my cheeks and back to my nose. I can smell a fire. Something is on fire. I smell toast and I heard this thing: I am having a stroke, because that is what happens. You smell toast.

I keep walking the walk, and my joints are starting to ache. They crack like rock.

The emotions of the wave have color. They change the visual patterns I see into blended collages, my retinas see watercolors. When I am mad there is a blend of faded red and orange on the walls. When I am afraid I see green. Up and down and faster and please and calm and pastels.

Around hours of pain. It could be days, but let us be realistic. This congenital mania begins the second I am awake one Monday morning, it can't last until Friday.

I well and my eyes widen slowly. I crawl onto the back porch and lay down. I look up at the sun and its beauty, I cry so slowly and reach out to it. I believe in God.

There is a pop somewhere in the neighborhood and I jump and run into the house and my heart is in my hands. I run really fast. Back door to front door and back door. Holy shit, my heart is in my hand and it is beating and all of the ventricles and veins and systems lead to their respective places through my epidermis. Oh Oh Oh Oh. No. My run goes to a jog, my jog takes about an hour and a half. I jog slowly from the front of the house to the back door. About fifty feet. So I can't feel my rattled, shaking heart, and the weightlessness in my stomach. Then I am able to walk for three hours. Then relative calm. I look out the window and I will kill whoever made that noise. I am not joking. How fucking inconsiderate, I will find them and I will tie them up in their basement.

They have to be close to here, that sound was only a couple of houses down. I open my front door with the brim of my hat real low and my eyes squinting out, that stupid sun, and I look to the left and then to the right. Then, I look back left and see a middle-aged woman leaving her town home. She is walking down her steps to her car, pretty from perfume and looking ready to be taken by gunpoint. Holy shit there is already a lot of blood in her hair. Wait, is there? Wait, there should be.

I picture running straight to her and grabbing her so hard by her hair and dragging her back into her fucking house and shoving a gun in her mouth. I take out the gun, What the fuck was that noise? Why the fuck did you do that? God Damn it you fucking cunt, I don't feel well.

A car door slams from the other direction and it startles me. My head flashes and I have to run back into the house to the back door. As I run back towards the front door I see the middle-aged woman driving out of my street, and I say a prayer. So should she.

I pace very fast, very fast with the waves at my brain stem. The top of my head has found peace and the monster is moving down my body. I cry cry so so hard hard. I put my back against a wall and bring my hands slowly to my face and I shake. I slide down the wall and feel not a hint of melodrama. I don't feel fake right now, I, I, I, don't want to do this anymore. I lay down where the wall meets the floor, and put my nose under the couch. There is no God…and I just want peace.

I feel so tiny, the world is too big for me. It doesn't need me, does it? Wait.

Never mind, holy shit my I can't swallow. I jump back up and start walking…very…s l o w l y. Calm Jay. The wave is back and lumping in my throat, alternating the throb. It is still in my head, everywhere, but not as bad. It circles around my shoulders, torn rotator cuffs. Then my chest is weightless. There is nothing in there, a ball is ponging back and forth in my ribs with echoes slamming into the bottom of my jaw.

Then the insanity, it hits my chest, my being heart, and soul. My heart hurts. That is not figurative. Once this is in you, it stays. I don't mean just now, just after this binge with withdrawal, it has been in me since my childhood, where I drained my young body of the positive responses in my rewards center. I actually didn't. My parents did this. Not one supportive word, not one "you are special," "you are my son," "I love you so so much," "you can do anything," "you can do anything." Every time I felt good about myself, my father fucking killed it. I hope he dies, I hope he –

My left arm has shooting pain down it. Oh, my left arm has its own waves coursing down to my fingertips, kissing my nails, flowing back up to my left midsection. The wave is pain and tingles and popping in my arm, and the main wave is spiraling in my chest cavity. I drank way too much. I drank over five gallons of vodka, IN EIGHT DAYS, DAYS, I am a horrible horrible man man. I must have met my drug dealer over twenty-five times, my stare draws in the glass to the front door, I have done more Coke than Freud. Who is that in the reflection? I hate him. Ah, another huge pain. It chokes me and I know that I am having a heart attack.

My lower back and upper thighs go numb, they tingle but when I put my hand there I can't feel them. It feels like a steak is attached to my hip. My ankle pops, it sends me reeling fuck this. My heart is working so hard, I can feel every pump and I would do anything for this to stop. Anything. I wish I had a gun, the creature moves back to my head, bouncing around, my chest aches, oh help. I am the worst person on earth. Boo hoo hoo hoo hoo, I heave and burst and my tears aren't salty and the wave is fully on in my stomach. It is so bloated, but it is empty, I haven't pissed or shit in days or eaten or done anything that my body adores me for. I have killed it, I have gone too far, oh my good bad god, look what I put people through…

I shock, like 120 volts goes through my body. Like I grabbed onto a contactor and pulled my hand back quick and my head shakes and my vision blurs momentarily and I sprint around my poor little carpet. The waves are in my upper legs, my stomach, my heart, and left arm. They hurt, call the cops. Fuck the cops. I hate the cops. I hate niggers, and spics, and jews, and crackers, and there is a fucking chink walking around my neighborhood. I fucking hate everyone, GOOOODD, I fucking hate people. I want people to die, and I want- shit a crack in me head. Was it just my vertebrae rubbing together from unhealthy days, no, no, no, it sounded like it was in the middle of my brain, not in my thoughts, but my tissue, a blood vessel, oh well.

    I run upstairs and look out the window and want to call out to those inferior races fucking up my street. I am frowning and rocking back and forth and try to swallow again but that chink won't let me. I can't feel my legs and I just tingle and I would rather die, I pick up the phone, hit 'phone', hit 9-1, hang up you pussy. Die at home like a man. And I crawl under the bed and scream for help and my yell reverberates through my body and I gotta get the fuck out of here, and I get up and smack my head on the bed frame and FUUCCKK YOOUU. God damn, who would design a bed like this and who the fuck would put it in this location in this stupid room, and I run back downstairs.

    At the bottom of the stairs my ankle gives and I fall into the door and whoever made those stairs is an absolute idiot and I hope someone steals his young daughter and rapes her and cuts her up-don't fucking think that, but the waves are hurting so bad and now they are all over my body, and they are moving so bad. They are toying with me and I am pacing and my feet, my awful feet. I should cut them off, I SHOULD CUT THEM OFF, they wouldn't ever walk me in to a liquor store again, and it hurts and I cry cry so hard for my poor family. I vomit fluorescent green, it pushes and gives birth out my mouth and it drains like and looks like antifreeze, but there is nothing in there to throw up, but it tastes like battery acid.

    My kneecaps are so sensitive, shattered little bowls holding my mangled cartilage, and I tap on one of them and the pain shoots up to my eyes and light bursts out of them filling the room. My waves are everywhere and in my calves and they hurt so badly but I have to keep running. I have to keep moving or I will start to think, I can't think, my brain won't work that way, it is too much stress, any little change, any little sign and I panic and I run. I am jogging but my ankles hurt. I am walking and my spine aches, and my whole body is capsizing and flushing and I am red and it has been over 36 hours and I have just been going around and around.

I am not tired I am so tired, I am just walking, and pops in my body and lights and stars in my vision, and chest pains, and breathing so hard, so hard. And fish scales for skin and trails behind of my dead flaking cells, and bloated face and stomach, and every inch hurts and every second lasts and every tear drops and the nightmare is real, and I can't, I can't, I can't.

I walk to the front door and head to the back door, and ouch, and ouch, and help, my whole body, shooting pains in my left arm and the linoleum and somewhe-

*   *   *

It starts when I open my eyes. I am freezing because I am sweating so badly. I wake with my back on the kitchen floor, I am staring up at the ceiling, at the paint patterns and uneven applications.

I don't panic, I don't have to jump, but I have to pull myself up. I get up slowly and look around, I scrape the crumbs from my eyes and nose. I blow my nose. I don't have to run, but I have to move. If I try to sit down, I look like I have mad cow disease, shaking and rocking, making grunts. I must pace around a little, and for the first time in two days, engage in thought.

The wave is still rolling, up and down. Synthetic, chemical, unkind, but easier. It drafts from the top of my head down to my chest, but it is slower. The pops are gone, no more loud whistles or gunshots in my tissue. The chest pain is there, but it lulls and doesn't surprise me with its loud interpretations. Jesus, what the hell has happened.

My joints ache really bad, really bad. I wonder how I got on the floor, if it was just a fall, or just a complete blackout, or something worse. But I am alive, I have made it through the death.

I am walking very slowly. My eyes feel slightly moist, they have closed for a while, and as such there are no more hallucinations. Just slight distortions in shapes, a lot of squinting. No more bugs on the carpet or human-shaped shadows darting across the room. No more crunching beetles. My eyes don't feel good, but they don't feel gone anymore. My nose throbs and aches but it doesn't feel like Mike Tyson hit me, it feels like I did a lot of cocaine and hurt a lot of tissue and am very grateful that I didn't OD. My mouth still tastes like ash, but at least it doesn't taste like smoke.

I am walking slowly, taking stock.

My tongue is abused, it is very sensitive to the sharp edges of the sharp teeth in my mouth, but screaming pain is no longer an issue. It just feels like I ate four bags of sunflower seeds in a row, and then sipped on turpentine. Like Van Gogh used to do. Just very coarse, there is no real taste to anything, not the air or my cheeks, but it is better than sensing the black hole density. My teeth don't feel like rocks, they actually feel soft. They feel like if I closed my mouth, and then clinched my jaw as hard as I could, they would all squish between my gums. I don't taste or smell anything anymore, and I feel a slight breeze as I walk that I know isn't really there, but it still feels nice. I am feeling again.

The cannon has stopped in my chest. I don't have weightlessness, emptiness, or incredibly shooting pains. Just throbbing, nobody is yelling in there anymore and the ball has stopped ponging, just whenever I feel my heart beat, it throbs a little. I have a headache, but no air pockets.

My chest cavity and stomach seem to be familiar again, nothing has ruptured, my stomach feels bloated, but not like an air balloon. Not that big. Just very uncomfortable. And I walk from the front door to the back door, but it takes me a lot longer, and in between my two destinations, I register what is around me. I blink, which wasn't happening. My intestines are clenched and angry, but ready to release.

My back and my thighs just ache. My back, I can kind of hear it, it is saying, "Jay, hello? Remember me? I hold your head to your feet? Can I please lay down?" Just a regular request from a tired part, did I just make a joke? I guess I did, the first one in days. My thighs feel very dense, but when I put my hand on them, they recognize that they are being touched. I can feel my hands too, nice, and my feet. My hands tingle like I have been sitting on them for a while, like maybe in a semi-healthy way. They are trying to accept my blood. Things are a bit slower. I still walk, but minutes feel like minutes, not like hours. The frantic pace of the wave and its intensity have drastically declined and I am able to form full sentences, even if out of partial ideas.

My neck really aches, but I can roll it and see how bad it actually it hurts. It is really sore. My fingernails, my long long fingernails, are yellow, but they're mine. They scratch my rough skin on my chest under my shirt and I see dandruff drop. My legs are aching so badly, so thoroughly. And there is a difference between the ache of a marathon aftermath, and an angry ache from an angry part. It is an undeserved, protracted contraction without the healthy exertion. My feet bottoms feel like kitchen-tile, just hard and smooth and unable to trace the fine contour of the soft carpet. They kind of stomp, but they are walking me around gently so I can lean my head back.

My ears aren't popping randomly or hearing subtle whispers, they aren't forcing me to spin around and ready my fists. They just listen to their heartbeat, and peacefully tell me of my outside sounds. My chest hurts, but it is bearable. My shins, my forearms, my buttocks, they all feel as though they have done the heavy lifting. They are tense and I flinch them occasionally just to know that they are okay.

My body from the inside out has calmed, not enough to sit, to focus on a book or on television, but I can peacefully walk back and forth so I don't have to hear my heartbeat or acknowledge my misery. My shoulders have dropped a little bit, settled back in to a familiar position. I am not clenching my jaw or twisting my back, ripping with the insanity of too much withdrawal.

I feel alternately hot and cold, I am sweating a little bit, and then I need to put on a long-sleeved-shirt. I am tired. I am tired but don't see sleep for at least another two days. I walk, and for the first time in a while, am able to open the front door, and leave it open, to see the sun beating down on the street. I can feel my eyes are still very sensitive to the bright shining light, but I let them take their time, they are not shocked or buzzing. I stand here and there, looking out a window or the front door for a second, out into the life that other people are living, and then I have to get back to moving a bit.

The phone rings, and it is bitter. It doesn't send me reeling, but my heart is pounding, and I am nervous to even look at it. I walk slowly away from it and let it finish its wondrous chime, it sounds like it is between two couch cushions. I wonder how many times it has rang lately, how many missed calls, how many new, unanswered text messages I will have, how many voicemai-not yet.

I keep walking back and forth trying to listen to the breeze and let the worm work its way out of me. There is an absolute impossibility of sipping water or taking in food, but I have a vague, fragmented memory of the last couple of days, and this, is actually better.

There are no more colors on the walls and no more violent patterns in any of the rooms, that is right, I am able to walk around the entire house. I have just acknowledged that, I am able to look out the back door, and, I really want a cigarette. But it is not yet time, time to choke on that. I keep walking, meandering, I hear sounds outside and they don't shock or startle me, I am a bit annoyed but am able to at least function enough to realize: I am a human being on planet earth, I don't feel well, but I am *not* the only one here.

I hear people and cars drive by slowly, I am able to close my eyes a bit and actually crack a tiny little smile. Hmph, it makes me feel better to know that people are out there living their lives while I am doing this to myself. To know that people may be out there driving their kids to some sort of practice. I hear a lawnmower start...I wonder what day it is. I wonder how long I will have to walk around, with nothing in my soul, nothing in my heart, and nothing in my brain, with marginal, well, comparatively marginal, physical pain, before I can lay down and get some sleep. I think it has been four and a half days since I had my final drink, I want my mind back. I want to be able to think. That is sort of funny, I am thinking about how I am not thinking, but it is true. I still can't think of anything outside of my body. When, when, when? This walk is really a drag, but it least it isn't the run. That is good news.

I walk for another couple of hours, nothing much changes, no new news. The exhaustion kicks in and my walk slows even more, more to a stammer. I close my eyes for thirty seconds at a time, it is getting close.

*   *   *

I wake up freezing again, drenched with sweat. It is hard to focus, I have a bad headache. My mouth is dry. I feel better, I feel better physically. But now, now, I must confront the emotional and intellectual hysteria I have created.

I think of this time, how did it start? What was the "trigger"?

The conceptualization of triggers should be left for the mid-grade and low-level addicts. Like one time, I cooked some chicken. After I removed the chicken from the tin foil resting in the glass oil pan, there was a residue of skin. Tracing the tenderness a black outline and rust, sizzling and bubbling with flavor that spoke to my soul, staring at me telling me to get a Bic pen, get a lighter, and get to work. What kind of tentative caution can I take when encountering such nightmares?

Everything is a trigger when you have used like I have. The second you open your eyes, for the rest of each day, you are doing something or seeing something or hearing something you have sensed when blasted into space. Free-base chicken crumbs, nothing in rehab warned me. I heard people in rehab talking about certain emotional states, certain people or places, certain songs, that would actually trigger them.

My triggers, all ten million of them, permeate the universe, are ubiquitous in my body, and I can't even understand where one begins and another ends, they are all there at all times. Every song, every meal, every moment.

Do I want an explanation for the way I have behaved? Here is the only answer anyone should ever give: I couldn't resist anymore. I wanted a break from the way that I felt all of the time. I wanted to get drunk. But, I absolutely did not want it to last this long. I actually thought, with no real concrete evidence, that it may just last that one night.

I look at my phone and I have 19 new voicemails, 46 missed calls, and 12 unread text messages. For someone who uses his phone for work, for home, and for everything else, one missed call over the course of a week is usually a lot. I wonder how long I have been gone.

I look at myself in the mirror, my god. My pupils are still massive, dilating at every movement. My beard runs from my chest hair to the top of my head, flattened and uneven, and totally ugly. My face is really swollen, pudgy and unfunny. My eyebrows are now my eyebrow. I am missing a front tooth. It was already broken, it was a temporary crown and it was one of my front teeth and I have had it for way too long. But it looks like I belong about eight hundred miles to the southeast. I hate the way it looks, I hate the way it feels, but it is not the first time.

My arms are tiny, I have no muscle-mass left. My hair is too long, I shave my head, as close as I can get, and this is an indicator of how long I have been gone. Including the horrible withdrawal, I would say just over two weeks.

I take a deep, deep breath; I cry. Not again.

I walk a little bit. Not because of the physical pain anymore, but because I am by nature a pacer. When I get really excited, when I am given or acquire new and useful information, I walk until it is fully analyzed. Fully accepted into its necessary cerebral areas. I walk a lot actually, so I do this now to think about everything.

Things were going so well. They always are. It doesn't matter if they are, or if they aren't or if they will, I took a sip, and the familiar reigned. I can't believe it is always the same, the same patterns and results. The same excuses, the same reasons, the same lies, the same anger, the same result, the same guilt, the same attempt, the same failure, the same begins again.

I walk around for a while. This time...it feels different. It isn't heavier, I don't feel any more depressed than I usually do. I feel...resigned.

If I had to guess, from that day that I honestly admitted that I was addicted, wanted to stop, to now; I would say that I have relapsed over two hundred times. Because I don't think that a relapse only occurs after you have sought help, or after you have had a maintained period of abstinence. Relapse happens when you realize that you don't want to drink or do any more drugs, ever again, but still do. It could be one hundred and fifty times. It could really be over a thousand. Really.

I feel no anger anymore. I am not mad at my parents, I am not mad at the world, I am not mad at myself. I have never felt this before.

There were good times.

I remember having so much fun. I remember this one time I was hanging out with my friends, there were four of us. We were in one of their parent's basements. One of the friends passed out and another one drew a swastika on his forehead. We went about our business for a while, laughing and making fun. Then, our friend came back in the room after he woke up and sat on the couch. We were all in synch. No one said anything but, "hey." After a while my friend goes, "You know, I read something like one out of every four young people in this country is a Nazi."

It lasted all night. I am not sure when he found out, but I am sure that my life has been filled with this kind of shit, the hilarious and totally exceptional. Not in a long time though. And I feel different.

I think and think and find it somewhere. Dormant and soft. Almost smiling, telling me: *You have spoken of me before, but something tells me this time we may get to know each other.* I don't even cry, but I am totally empty.

Then...I know...I can't do this anymore. I have lost all hope. Let me tell you...when you really admit that actually, honestly, powerfully, and pathetically, you know that you are going to give up, you don't tell anyone.

I keep sighing, cursing myself for being so sick. The gigantic misery and disproportionate guilt are more than I can carry; the weight has become of greater suffering than the value of continuing. There is just nothing left inside of me.

I have never felt anything like it. I am not angry with anything. I am not even sad. It is strangely peaceful. I knew it was going to end. I cry, but I am not hard inside, I am not thinking of what I have done. I am not thinking of my pain. I feel almost liberated; I am not happy, trust me, I am not happy. I am not ecstatic, and I can't even begin to understand what it will do to my family. To my friends. To Mya. To maybe everyone that has ever met me, or believed I am unique. I have been in rages and funks, yelled about it over the phone, spoken to therapists about it. I have threatened it, wrote about it, and I *am* sad. I am sad over a young life, a life that carries so much potential, so much beauty. But I am not sad about death itself. I am sad that maybe my life could have made a difference, but I have proven to myself that I won't ever live that life.

It doesn't feel like a decision I am making on any intellectual or spiritual or emotional level, it feels like I have simply lost my imagination. My ability to believe. My ability to connect with what makes me happy in any way. I have tried mood stabilizers, I have tried anti-depressants, I have tried writing and reading, I have tried working really, really hard. I have tried rehab, I have tried psychiatry, I have tried athletic training, I have tried saying no, I have tried AA, I have tried meetings of all sorts, I have tried loving and laughing, I have tried letting a decade pass, I have tried it all. Nothing seems to be able to take away the desperation. I like my life, but I like it momentarily better when I am high. Then I absolutely hate it for a while.

The sadness; the electrical misfiring and consequent malfunctioning; the chemical toxicity; the emotional paralysis; the moral degradation; the social isolation; the skin I am in belongs to someone else; I reluctantly admit, it was not my time to be here. The only real fear of death I have ever had is of reincarnation.

So I go see Mya. I see her and feel remorse about lying to her face. I tell her I think I am okay. I feel like hell, and we watch some movies. I cry while I watch Mya sleeping, and I whisper goodbye to her, and tell her everything, hoping her spirit will understand. She deserves twenty pages here of explanation, but I am tired. I whisper to her that I have had enough.

Ray Charles once said in a song, and I have heard it before, but not in his beautiful melody, that time heals all wounds. Well...what happens when time stops?

It is like the earth is literally sucking, atmospherically, the shit out of me. The diarrhea, the eating, the sipping on water, the crying, the small physical symptoms haven't stopped, but I am sure that they will.

I have learned, from this condition: perspective, humility, patience, and courage. And wish desperately that I had held on to enough of these to believe that I could stop all of this. But I do believe that the pain that I bring my family when I do decide to do this, this horrible thing, will one day go away. But this...this never will. This feeling of exasperation.

This feeling of not feeling. It is simply too much.

(THE REVOLUTION)
18..

Race is the genesis of culture, in the end, and culture is the genesis of racism. Personal dispositions, grooming habits, artistic tastes, clothing, and food, and other things are all effects of culture. If culture, and the people within it, that help constitute that definition, is produced because of race, the race of human beings in their particular epidermal evolutions, and sexes, then sexism, racism, and classism, by definition, are all completely counterintuitive. It is all some weird self-hate.

The subtitled revolution that remained in my head for so long was incoherent. It worked like that, it was backwards. I liked the word, and the association with violence. I enjoyed its ring, its purity, what it could possibly mean. What, in the connotative and denotative meanings of the word and its relevance and its power to demand emotion, it could actually be. I could really relate to nothing.

But with clarity, after much time, it *is* revolution that I am thinking of. Actually, two revolutions.

Hiccup.

They were real, but expressed with detachment and ignorance. When I was using constantly, I had transformed my surroundings into good versus evil. Black versus white. Sick versus healthy. My mentality was very divisive, very confrontational.

One was traditional. Social revolution, the one I have selectively and strangely used as a talking point, has always generated from my feelings about racism. About our sociological imperfections within our national framework; my feelings about equality; the contrasts in our lives; the polarity I see in each of us, in each neighborhood, in each community, in each county, in each state. The way I was lied to in school, concealing the truth is no different than not expressing it, and it left me furious.

The other revolution, the personal revolution I was really unaware of, was one that I did not expect. Or desire, or welcome. The change within the "I." The cellular revolution. One that took me in, and washed me clean. The overturning change that comes simply with the passing of time, and thus, the changing and shifting of the forms and expressions of our dreams.

A couple of years ago I was in Downtown Denver, but I was sober. It was a beautiful day, but I was racked with pain. It was a day that I used to have all of the time. A desperate depression sinks in after a slight anger, then an all-day exhaustion. Someone had said something mildly offensive, I raged with the power of way too much dedication, and then became upset with myself. Angry with my anger, and I became sad.

I found myself standing by the intersection that serves as a small skid row in our biggest city. I think of Skid Row as an entire community, housing, functioning standards of respectable behavior policed by the intolerant and partially insane. This intersection is a block in that corrupted city square. People were crammed into a cement public park bordered by three major one-way streets that close it in a triangle. It is across from a mission, a well-intended fantasy for those that have been made comfortable by the freedom or misery of anonymity.

They seemed collected, posing and spraying, and I stopped across the street for just a minute to register the nastiness of our lost. They froze and huddled and engaged in unimaginable activities. They smiled, they actually played and interacted and loved and hustled as one organism. And then they broke apart, confetti whirlwinds of paper and loud spit and bleeding gums. Then they contracted back, an inflatable crowd sinking back into its natural form.

I wondered what kind of help any of these monsters would be willing to accept; these people are probably too far gone. That does not mean that they don't matter, but I have spoken to many of them, and most of them are where they want to be. They have become accustomed to the lonely desert, or are schizophrenic or chronically addicted. Not all homeless people are lost, and all I could think of was adult literacy.

These men and women are representatives, the floor of the market. But I still desperately love them, even if they are upset with me for wanting to help people who don't need no help. The target demographic for the changing of the sociological vanguard is right above them, and goes all the way through the middle class. The upper class in America is too small of a percentage of the people, and too white, I am afraid I would have to leave them behind. I will never give them a free hand-out, those people who use the system to their advantage just disgust me.

Hiccup.

After approaching the crowd and asking if they had any cocaine, I left, and went on to the next innocuous event in my life of which I have absolutely no memory. I was depressed, consumed with the random inconsolable. Confused about the revulsion the homeless community felt when I asked them for drugs in that triangle, and in all other shapes.

I had 'championed' the rights for the homeless since I understood the quantity of people who were homeless here, but there was something I did not know about them. They have homes and communities, they have standards of living, they are gentle and vicious and just just people. And each and every one looked at me with either wonderment or complete horror when I asked them if they had coke or dope. I did not know at the time, that although alcoholism is extremely common in the homeless community, that a lot of them had no desire for hard drugs, and considered such impulsions to be a characteristic of people on a lower level of the human hierarchy. The irony was instructive. Maybe I should have waited until it was late at night.

This was near the time when I first went to Capitol Hill to find drugs. Broadway was so fast so close to me, and I felt the same. Loud. I needed to find drug dealers, not people without homes. A change of venue. The truly homeless, or really, houseless, were strangely less tolerant than any one group in my life had previously been, these men I disturbed with my insane requests, and I adored them for that. They had almost nothing, by way of possessions, but I found they cared curiously more about their little collection of things than most do about the condition of their homes. They organize and itemize and categorize their bundles and are as fierce about its protection as we are about private school security. It was funny, and terribly shameful. I had no choice but to move on, knowing that I had been rejected thoroughly by people who have been thoroughly rejected. Even in the suburbs, there were so many times in so many places that I was to ask a middle-class prototype for where I could find something hard, to have them politely and almost apologetically say that they didn't know. A couple of the homeless people that I asked were to look at me with an anger or disgust that I have received from only one person on this planet before them. They looked at me like my father used to when I was young, which is probably why I was so embarrassed when they did.

Capitol Hill would eventually serve as my default location to find whatever I wanted, but on this day, as I drove away from 'the triangle' and leaned right to get onto the major highway, the Interstate

25, there it was: I was beginning to devolve. Going from logistical considerations for new standards of brotherhood, wondering how I could help, spawned by the lost in the concrete jungle, to being only concerned about my lack of happiness. I didn't really even know how I had gotten to my car, or from where I had wandered. I went from looking for drugs in the wrong place while thinking of social revolution, to finding drugs pathologically and cursing the warfare that was constantly inside of me. I was beginning to experience the hopeless absence of any physical feelings of joy, when I looked up. It was in black spray paint, on the side of an overpass:

WE NEED A NEW HERO

In that moment of duality, almost randomly as I saw that, I realized that drug addiction and alcoholism had been partially responsible for the intensity of my social consciousness. That I was projecting a need for revolution into society because of the revolution I was constantly experiencing biologically and philosophically. The forced, internally systemic changes made me resentful, and I was finding the conflicts everywhere, even when they were unnecessary.

I was being overturned constantly, and was unaware of how powerful it was.

I realized I was longing for a new hero too, and knew that I hadn't thought of agrarian reform, nothing had crossed my mind about property rights. I didn't think of the redistribution of wealth, or the nationalization of banks or any other private sector. I had no program for the eradication of sexism and racism. I never thought of political reorganization, democracy, coup's, but I knew what I meant. I meant that something was wrong, and wanted change for its own sake. There was a Communist inside of me, but I was and had been thinking of my personal revolution, my need for the world to be okay; no more conquests of outer-space, just the exploration of my inner-space.

Even as I studied revolutions, I was using their projected references regarding contemporary American society to try to have impact. I had not thought of any of the practical or bureaucratic necessities of revolution. Of gaining the trust and support of the future proletariat, trying to include freedom of study, freedom of choice of work, freedom of the exchanging of ideas and of some type of electorate, ideally applied within socialist principles. Of abolishing individual wages, suspending independently owned property; thinking of just and minimalist leaders who live exactly as the people they govern do, a joy of work and community and innovative progress as one ridiculously idealistic people.

Nothing was explored, just expressed.

Hiccup.

I hadn't even considered that there were revolutions that did not have to be socialist. How pathetic.

I imagine if I was running around on fire, hunting for the next violation of my humanity, I would have driven right by that spray-painted phrase. If I were really high, I would have had other worries. Maybe grunted. But that was a day that I was able to resist, or to come up empty. Like so many of the good days in my life, the monster wasn't overpowering, just squirming in my chest and stomach, looking for a way up. But I kept him down. After I was denied, I moved on.

Then, later, to escape my own reality, I started thinking about what the external revolution was. About what it is that I am talking.

And I realized, using the first person plural, is an easy way to avoid direct responsibility.

We have to recognize the disparity between our ideas and our actions. I have to recognize the immaturity, the foolishness in which my "revolution" requires me to indulge. My vocalization of social revolutionary executions began to sound to me, well, revolting. All that it boils down to is that I absolutely hate seeing my brothers and sisters in rotten housing, in rotten clothing, in rotten foods, in rotten moods. I do not have to employ such language because that kind of revolution is not what I dream of anymore. It is not in fatigues and force, in bombs and buildings, in revisions and invasions, it is in the people and the power, in the attitude and arrogance. It is inside me, listening; not acting.

It is in the spirit of Bernie Glassman:

"When we bear witness, when we become the situation – homelessness, poverty, illness, violence, death – the right action arises by itself. We don't have to worry about what to do. We don't have to figure out solutions ahead of time. Peacemaking is the functioning of bearing witness. Once we listen with our entire body and mind, loving action arises."

It is that individually, apart from the total whole, we enjoy the idea that people are inherently good. They are just trying to be happy and avoid suffering like us, so we treat them well. I try. But when they become part of that whole, that larger group, the festering incantations, that when alone we ignore, come alive and they employ them without reservation.

Like *The Lucifer Effect,* I see that as a corollary, when we become ugly as a group, by the transit of properties, we become ugly, as individuals. It is that the citizen and the society are one.

It is in Thomas Paine saying that his country is the world and his religion is to do good. It is in the sick people decrying and shouting about the world's poverty, about the conditions everywhere, and forgetting to mention them here.

It is in this:

I don't like these cold, precise, perfect people, who, in order not to speak wrong, never speak at all, and in order not to do wrong, never do anything.

-Henry Ward Beecher

My misconceptions of revolution, mixed with chaotically angry amounts of hate for people who do not care, brought me to these things that are much more complex. It is in being away from the visualizations of actual killing, of taking life and extinguishing ideas, to believing in the power of the proliferation of knowledge, and in our true desire to do good. It is believing in "we" ourselves, singularly, that our own lives can be revolutionized. I do not wish for mechanical equipment, for guns and technology, but for an adjustment of the way we study, and the way we apply our wisdoms.

Woe is me, I am interested in everything. Everything about us and here and there fascinates me.

It is in the almost coherent nature of my thinking; but the absolutely scattered unclear expression of it.

Hiccup.

I am not saying I am any better or more intelligent than anybody because of some effortlessly inquisitive nature, I am just saying that I have never understood apathy or separateness. It is that what I have done with my studies can be done by anyone, and I am scared that most will never be here, they will never throw away their insulated life-jackets. There is so much knowledge and wisdom to be gained and retained by engaging your mind, by reading everything you can get your hands on, by truly listening to people, and the best part is that your lineage will be forever improved. You can genetically pass down improvements to your neuroscience and temperamental disposition, and you can teach your young all that you have learned. So they can one day know too that with the proper perspective, the idea that any of us are at all disconnected in any way from each other is a complete fiction. You can hand down the idea that Socrates first taught me: I now know enough to know that I know nothing.

It is this:

If I study and listen enough to people, my revolution will come true. *My* revolution. The change inside me that will come physically, emotionally, temperamentally, intellectually, and spiritually, in tiny and orgasmic ways, and will teach me that any kind of revolution, any kind of condensed evolution, is a powerful notion.

I do not believe exactly what I used to believe. I believe a moment of love, even in a bad man, brings worth to a life. I no longer believe that that moment, is too little too late.

At some point, my ideas went from building new nations, cessation, blind want, to the little things we do that generate my feelings about society at large. I view most people as harmless, but uninterested. I didn't used to.

There are grown men who dress their homes, cars, and closets in local football team garb, or who organize an entire month around a college basketball tournament; these men that dedicate themselves only to those that they are familiar with, those that submit to localism, are who I have been noticing. I didn't used to.

Hiccup.

There are women who have been abused, emotionally castrated, who are selling their bodies out of complete economic destitution, feeding habits, forgotten by the society of men who have always sworn to protect them. They are who I have been thinking of.

All the lonely little children, shuffling their diapers into drug-addicted streets, late at night, with no one to mal-adjust them, finding ways of being so on their own. Those are the people I think of. And the people in power who claim to love, but show only bright white smiles. Politicians are business men, who go into politics. Plato would not be surprised. I think of the practical ways in which "the system" can be changed, the social system, the system of thinking of many different people. Which would mean the adaptation of the political landscape.

I have no more dreams of marching through the woods, being interviewed importantly. Sometimes I think of just leaving.

Chuck Palahniuk wrote that first your parents give you your life, then they try to give you theirs. What I finally have realized is that I don't want their lives, I don't want the mental separation of our beautiful peoples into domesticated, arbitrary groups, complete with irrationally racist sentiments. I don't want to think like our parents did. I also do not want to line up anyone against a wall anymore, unless it is to ask some questions.

Some shifting and changing in my dreams, came when I was able to abstain. To abstain from self-indulgence, to clear the slate, to see as me. It will come again and again. It is so much more base, and so much more important than a threatening, violent, political overturn. It is so much more difficult and so much more profound to invoke change through kindness, and through the presentation of more satisfying paths. Through wisdom.

To force people to look at themselves, by showing them myself.

It is in a life of love, it is not in me constantly debating my level of revolutionary commitment. It is in me always remembering that I do not know what brings people into my life so briefly, and how every single encounter I have with people will have an effect on who I am. It is not in me passing judgment, feeling incredibly sick, thoughts spinning in cyclical patternized neuroses. It is not in me deciding theoretically who lives and who dies when I "take power", but in the little ways I am able to be sincerely open with people, genuinely listening, smiling as they tell me things they don't tell themselves.

It is always in me recognizing and respecting and making love to the idea that on any given afternoon, when I am truly sober, I can be sure that time passes with more fluidity and the next day is always only so far away. That people are around, that they and myself count. The only real question is, what will I do with that day?

It is not in me being up and down, turning knobs and hitting switches and yelling mayday, thinking of people as failures for their lack of complete and unbounded compassion. Where it is, is in today, in asking questions: Can we get outside of our heads? Is it possible to see ourselves from the outside, as small and as great and as funny as we are?

Is it possible for us to feel good and big, feel important and needed and special, and also recognize how little we really end up as?

Hiccup.

Because my revolution demanded a hope for experiences out of the extraordinary, a blind desire to be part of any events that drew attention. It was wrong. It was me on my knees in a hallway, trying to give CPR to a dead man.

I was in a bender, and a thump hit outside the door of the apartment I was in, out in the hallway.

A minute later someone knocked, a neighbor who had given me cocaine on many occasions. He looked at me, wavering behind the opened door, "Do you know this dude?"

The coke man and I got down, he began chest compressions, I began mouth to mouth. Another drunk, in this dingy collapsible hallway, called the police.

The man from the thump gurgled and death soup bubbled into my mouth, there was fluid in his lungs. When the medics got there, they said he may have been alive when we started, but he didn't make it. It wasn't anyone's fault, it appeared that he was an addict who overdosed. I went back into the apartment and involuntarily tried to join this young man. It was the second person that I watched die, from exactly what I was pumping into me. I wanted to know where he got what got him.

And strangely, I felt involved. There was something there, something seminal and real. Away from all of the mundane and monotonous days, I actually felt more alive close to this death than I had in years. Not in comparison, but in vitality. Everyone was stunned, wondering about the young man's life, being nice with each other, and I felt like a delusional revolutionary. I felt like I could look someone in the eyes, and say 'yes, I know that the drug war is a war, because I have seen the casualties.' It is in this attitude being sad to me now, pathetic; no longer is it compelling, how sick that is.

What of my thinking is revolutionized from this experience? I both feel an internal change, in my personal revolution, and a change in the way I see the need for change in society. I will die just like him if I don't stop, and it isn't cool to die for nothing. It isn't revolutionary just to be close to tragedy.

These events had become normal and the spinning and confusion and madness had confused my own morality. I was begging for distinctions: What is worse, helplessness or hopelessness?

What is worse, me being surrounded by people falling down, dying from my particular poison? Or me being away, imagining the pain. If I run from it, am I giving up?

It is not in me being excited about situations that test my manly constitution, it is in me recognizing that a human life, for whatever reason, was just taken.

It is in me helping either way. If someone is hopeless, my job is to reach down, to show through the soft and critical eyes I maintain, that no matter how far gone you are, there is hope. Where there is helplessness? Well, that is easy...me being sober is priority number one. Anything I have to do to stay sober. And after that, I must rage against the dying of the light and always try to bring help, in any futile way I can.

'Ideas on a revolution', in the singular personal meaning that applies to myself and my development, is not a phrase about a social movement, but cellular change. Change that occurs on quantum mechanically small levels; change which, through dedication and routine and dedication, can find a way of making me so much level. Change that comes through a gigantic love of the self, and its innovative potential.

I have long thought about personal revolutions, about the massive overturns and structurally systematic changing of established orders in our daily functionality.

I have long pictured becoming calm, or on strange days imagined the non-existence of addiction in my life, and dreamed of simply keeping my ideas revolving around the aggregate.

I have long pictured my professor saying – "That stuff happens *because* you are contracted, and that's why you notice." We are speaking of a theoretical man, a man who steps into a street on a patch of ice, noticing it before he steps on to it. Contracting himself, holding his balance into his chest. So he slips *because* he is aware that he may slip. And I say to my personal professor, "that isn't what I am concerned with. What I wonder about is what will happen to this man the next time he is put there, now that he knows his protective contraction had everything to do with his fall?"

Hiccup.

Randomly, non-important, philosophical think-tank conversations. Pointless. These are what I have pictured, moments like these.

Like who coined the phrase 'to coin the phrase'?

It is, this concept of revolution, about a normal future.

It is not in me being hard, being rigid about the survival of the fittest, telling people too bad, you just aren't good enough. Not caring about those people, the ones with feelings.

But it is in me believing in the acceptance of our limitations. What we can not succeed or exceed.

I can see what my revolution has brought me. A bigger heart, a colder intelligence. I can see what going through this long process has done to me, with so much internal change.

So no, I don't think that a man in a wheelchair should apply, or be considered for, stocking boxes. I think he should roll up his mobile office and take a call. And so foolishly and arrogantly I believe he should be happy to have such a purpose, an occupation in which he can excel.

And I do not think handing out handicapped parking passes to overweight people who have been diagnosed as clinically obese is going to be healthy for anyone, and I secretly resent people whom are very fat, as though they don't have enough on their plate. Puns and sayings and expressions sometimes fit like they want to. Overweight people have addictions that are so obvious, it is unfair.

I don't enjoy plastic covers on couches, or stupid furry car-seat liners, fooling ourselves into thinking that we are doing anything but preventing ourselves from being reminded of our own struggle with chronology and dust. Or tough-guy daywalkers on the corner packing their hard-packs to pass the aggressive time.

What is this revolution? It is not in me distrusting every politician, always. Until, personally, they prove to me they deserve any other considerations.

And I do not typically enjoy religious people. When using, I have a hate for everyone who believes in something so ridiculous. Not religion itself, not theology, but the morons who apply it so counterintuitively. I feel so jealous, I don't have God, I have to go through this alone. I feel as though no matter what, when I am around someone who is vocally and unnecessarily pushy with religion, I am around a monster-type hypocrite.

It is in me at times reading *The Idiot,* and laughing at how Dostoevsky can say so poetically that at least two-thirds of all human beings are completely untalented.

But...but. It is also in me knowing, knowing that I have generalized and been disgusted, but if I were to meet any group of people in any of these situations individually, I am positive I would gently smile to welcome them in, and listen with the soul.

It is strange being okay with your duality. Your own contradictions.

In an interview not too long before she passed away, Kanye West's mother, who had been a university professor, quoted Walt Whitman. She was asked in some way about Kanye's contradictions, the hypocrisy in his music. She said, "I am reminded of Walt Whitman...who once said 'I contradict myself? Fine, I contradict myself. I am large, I have multitudes...'" That strong, beautiful woman referenced the sublime, the way of saying something that has captured an idea so perfectly, the rest of men that come thereafter should continue to use these same words in this same order to say the same thing. As I do about the changes in my mood and attitude, in the matter of fact, the absurd, and the space that is produced when I scatter rude. I am constantly borrowing ideas from other people, who can say things without such hate.

My value systems, my idiosyncrasies, my angry little appetizers, don't feel as though they were given to me genetically.

The things that were most truly passed down to me by my parents are the way I look, and my temperament. My general, overall cynicism. The ways, the directed frowns, are all mine. Of course, all of that is completely understated, but I believe most of my social and intellectual values have come from my studies, and my experiences. Like everyone's. So in that way, my parents did directly impact me for many years because my experiences revolved around them for so long. But I did not just inherit them.

My value systems seem to be malleable.

When I think of very serious threats, not the bi-monthly guffaw, the insult thrown at the local bar trailer-rat, the girl in the seat with not so many teeth, threats that are real like poverty, I obviously get much more serious. And that's when I know what my values are.

When I think of other things, I get even more serious: forced polygamy; child prostitution; torture. But some days, when I am thinking of only me, thinking about a lot of things I thought previously were very important, but now I know are small, I still refuse to apologize. To apologize for taking seriously almost all things.

Some things, for instance, I don't know what they mean, but I do pity people. I do feel bad for people, individually, obsessing over trivialities, changing clocks as they change moralities, content with the simple boredom we hope not to break with tragic news. And, collectively.

There is no way to think the following and not sound extremely aloof. It doesn't feel like it comes from such a place, but it could. I feel like humanity, with all of its eloquence and imperfection, wishes to be remembered not for its innovation, but for its rigidity. It takes so long for things to change for the good.

The presence of arrogance in that, I suppose, is in speaking of humanity in the third person. But I know that I am a part, a small part of the wondrous evolving whole.

The human race has given me fascinating things to read about. To learn about as to codify my system of beliefs. And I am part of Shakespeare and Stalin, Einstein and Hitler. Gandhi and Genghis. I am a product of and a contributor to Soweto, and to the abolishment of slavery and President Barack Obama. If the two symmetric dualities are necessary for our existence, I am then ready. If people, including myself, could ever meet their potential and treat each other with generosity and overwhelming honesty, with intense dignity, it would be a boring morning to wake up on. It seems necessary for both of the parts, black and white, to exist, for the whole to have meaning. I wish that it didn't.

I am a part of the cynical philosophical school, I don't think it is possible for us to meet our potential. That is okay, as long as we try. But I do not think we will ever have to concern ourselves with how *else* to spend our national defense budgets.

We will war, and we may extinguish ourselves.

Psychologists have told me that this is unhealthy. That the forced acknowledgment of all of our atrocities can bring only despair. That so much distracted and fragmented concentrations are harmful. I have heard that from so many people. But I disagree. Thoroughly.

If it weren't for the lonely, annoying people who consume my focus, the gifted and long passed away, I may lose all revolutionary focus.

That focus that has brought revolt against my learned, oppressive dispositions. There was an upheaval and condensed evolution. I soaked up everything until I was eighteen, drenched myself, wrung out for ten years, and somehow get to appreciate myself and all of our stupidities that much more. I get to be further along, philosophically and intellectually. I get to evaluate myself, in every way, on every day. Even if physically I am well behind all others my age.

I get to go to all-white rehabs and use my writing simply to expose and exploit my personal viewpoints without feeling guilty. I get to be free.

I get, at least, to see myself as a source and object of constant change, of perpetual revolution. Trotsky would be proud.

I get to tell you one powerful, immutable truth: I will not be had for any price. Because I will eternally fear my permanent conscience, not the temporary imprisonment of my physical being, or the fleeting completion of sociological privilege. I will always care, and try to will myself more complete.

*   *   *

The American ghetto is a maddening tragedy. The afterbirth of slavery, the wretch, the breathing and heaving cities that collect the most cleverly oppressed men and women in history.

The middle-class is a confused demographic, egos and e-mails and the dead-center money.

This is a more pronounced vision of the social "revolution": Pamphlets and flyers and telephone poles in South Central and Queensbridge and Aspen and everywhere, plastered and pasted and perfect: LIBERATION.

A call for the mobilization of the movements and the parades and the smart, of the boardrooms and the dogs and the suits, a consolidation. A far cry from free love and integration, the times when the best way to stand up was to sit in.

This movement is driven by the rage, the rage that does not allow you to sit and be beaten, by anything real or metaphorical, to be shut up or shut down, to be violently interacted with.

This rage you must feed and encourage, brutally cage and torture at times, the rage that comes from "universal growing pangs" and so many promises. The rage that comes from the stabbing songs of inequality. The raceless rage; the transcendental anger of those who can no longer be ignorant of such injustice, in such proximity. The rage that has no boundaries, no color lines, no cultural or geographic definitions.

The real revolution is the desperate and aggressive demand for an informed, true, just, loving consciousness.

What I am talking about is self-realization. All demographics, all classes. All people sharing common histories. I am talking about a universal mind. A rage that can make a miracle, and have us hearing with our heads and our hearts. Upright creatures who lower themselves lovely, who lay and listen to the loudness. To the people so close to home, who are also yelling enraged.

Yelling inside, too fed up to take it out on anyone in particular. People like me, who see the fast-paced cyanide being bred in our brains.

A focused, almost restrained rage that is not an abstract, reactionary, junkyard ferocity. A rage that is concentrated, harnessed, compassionately directed in the meaningful goal of global dominance. The dominance of decency.

An exemplary rage:

A man once went to the Mahatma, Mohandas, with a rage that was unequivocal, bursting from his chest. He was deeply furious. Pain unbounded. He told the open one, the greatest listener, that Muslims had come to his house and killed his child. His rage bubbled from his pores, his little boy and his little life were both dead.

Gandhi looked at him with the most beautiful Hindu and Indian dedication, and said that he had the solution. The remedy for this sickly father was to go and find a little boy, a little boy who is without parents. One that he could raise as his own, that he could raise not to hate. And the boy must be a Muslim.

A rage that jumps off the page.

Hiccup.

One definition of a revolution is an overthrow or repudiation; the thorough replacement of an established government or political system by the people governed. This type of institutional corroboration is not necessary, the institution is an effect of the greatest of causes, the political system follows the personal sacrifice. Self-imposition. The putting of people and principles *before* politics and policy.

This revolution is an ideal, the ridiculous, the nonsensical compassion required for something like non-violent non-cooperation.

A resistance of blame placement, of pettiness and separation. A rejection of factions and peoples and skins. The All.

What I am talking about, really, is reinvention. I know that now.

Forget highway appropriations, market interest rates, agrarian reform, literacy campaigns, investment. Forget economics, agriculture, technology, especially politics.

Forget infrastructure. Water, electricity, food, police, protection, trash clean-up. Forget the governors and mayors and the president.

This is an internal revolution, a cerebral one, caused and dictated by the people, for the people, about the people. Even, yes, upper-class people.

Evolution, condensed.

Hiccup.

It must begin with self-identification.

With the accepting of responsibility and the negation of expectations. No storming into classrooms screaming at teachers. No more frivolous lawsuits. No more right-wing conservatism. No racism, none. No militarism or propaganda. No more business ruling politics. No more left-wing weakness, no more endless dissolution through impractical togetherness. No more communism, no more rampant individualism. No more capital controlling the country. No more campaigns based on accusation. No more politics based on moral cleanliness, rather than the demonstration of knowledge. No more soccer-moms. No more denying of empirical evidence for the existence of evolution. No more arrogant atheism, no more condescension. No more biblical moralism, no more science without emotion or spirit. No more allowing the small minority, insane and radical, to dominate the landscape of the majority.

'The people' will believe in equal rights for gays, all races, women. The people will finally embrace the domination of the sensibilities that control the movements of most of us here. No more excusing superficialities as necessities for consumer marketplace productivity.

No more rhetorical confusion.

No more rhetoric, no more hyperbole. No more of this.

Hiccup.

Because I despise the dolts and dufuses who suggest being against the war in Iraq is the same as not supporting the soldiers. The insolence and ignorance it requires.

No more blind faith in imperialism, colonialism. Age-old words with age-old concepts still applicable today. No more waving the flag without understanding what it represents. No more totally revisionist history. Things are always somewhere in the middle.

No more torture…no more torture.

No more elitist, aristocratic, fringe rule; religious impetus. No more Pat Robertson or Jerry Falwell followers. No more idolizers of Richard Dawkins.

No more lack of study, lack of real comprehension of what this country is truly involved in. No more judgment of people you just don't understand.

No more Reagan, no more being one of two countries in the world to support a South African, Apartheid government. No more Iran Contras. At least, no more lying all of the time about all of it.

No more voting in the United Nations solely to protect our economic and militaristic obsessions. No more voting with Israel no questions asked.

No more living inside illusions of qualitative progress, no more denying the hunger and poverty that exist right here, right next door.

No more excuses for ruthless criminals.

Hiccup.

No more redneck nationalism. Ironically, nationalism should be reserved for people who have had no cultural or philosophical or political history of their own. It is an empty concept. National pride, an attempt at unifying a people with an intended goal of taking care of each other, is good. Waving a flag, trying to dominate the regional landscape, feeling some exclusive right to enjoy this society, xenophobia, is insanity. Any country, established and economically autonomous, should be compelled to regard their philosophy as internationalist or global. Nationalism should be band after the first fifty years of the establishment of a nation, when it is needed for identity. After that, it is just masturbation. No more confusing what national pride is, with what personal gratitude for accidental birthplace should be. If we have confidence in the people we are, we do not need to spend any time telling others. We are Americans, thankful and simple.

We are Western, no doubt about it, capitalist and democratic. But we can strive to be better.

From my understanding, the concept of suffering avoidance is Eastern. We need that, with an edge. Confucianism; excellence; moral law; the cultivation of the order of the self.

The West is about the perfection of the Self, and the East is about the removal of it. There has to be a way to integrate the two ways of living.

Perhaps a Western application of the Eastern concept of Yin and Yang, opposites not only existing in contradiction to each other, but needing each other to exist at all. Taking the picket lines and the protests to the debate halls, off of the violent corners crowded with police. Committing to education and debate. Taking the venom to the voting booth, to each other's senses, and living with the results. Acknowledging the right we all have to stand center stage. Noticing that without Republicans, the country would fall apart. And without Democrats, the country would grow stale and die.

Hating no one.

Hiccup.

This revolution is a commitment to non-pacification. And non-violence. The government can't allow enough alcohol or drugs or food or gambling or shopping malls to take our concentrations off of what is important: The health and prosperity of our people, and all people. There are no programs that can reach out to inner-city neighborhoods. There are no education stipulations, no public assistance functions, no labor laws, no gun bills to be passed, that can touch the self. No expectations. No being quiet. No separation of the self from the whole.

There exists here, already: The freedom to assemble with those that feel the same. The freedom to study whatever subject it is that will set you free. The freedom of information exchange. The freedom to speak your mind and disseminate what you have learned. The freedom to create Art, Art that reflects the times and represents the hopes and failures of all of this wisdom.

There exists here, in this country, the greatest and freest in the world, the ability for rapid change. Rapid revolution.

Hiccup.

The difference between change and evolution is that evolution is always a process; change can be manipulated, evolution must be directed. For even if you believe you stand in opposition to something, your contrast contributes to its identity and longevity. Your contrast helps it to exist. Yin and Yang.

No more road rage. No more assumptions.

Inclusionary philosophies.

If you are poor, no more presumptions about the attitudes of the rich. If you are rich, no more ignoring of the poor.

I've seen these men, bent to the street with arthritic hopes, poor in oh so many ways, resenting the money and not wanting any. With 360 degrees of addiction and mental illness, full of hate, limping to their next great failure. All they want is normalcy, or maybe just a cigarette.

I've seen these men, walking tall, straightening their ties walking into the tenth- story office, seeking success. They want to take care of their families, not to live in greed or to be steeped to their eyeballs in crystal. They care too.

I've seen these women, prostituting their bodies or their souls, or their minds or their hearts, selling themselves short, collapsing in grief wishing their men understood the true meaning of fidelity. Wishing that society hadn't short-changed them, wishing they didn't have to pick up the John's with the quirks in their smiles.

I've seen these women, these strong protectors of the family, these Goddesses, raising the children and doing it out of care, expecting only love in return. They drive from here to there and bring the kids everywhere, and are still strong enough to hold onto their own dreams.

Hiccup.

I've seen sweeping generalizations. I've seen sleepy mid-afternoons and riotous nights.

I see my brothers and sisters sitting on the concrete blocks in front of the Post Office laughing off the beginning stages of sickness. I've seen CEO's cry away guilt, and donate a lot of money.

I've seen The All. The revolutionary idea that from far enough away, we are all one organism. From the sky all you see is land and ocean, and know not of our little quibbles.

I have seen both ends of the social spectrum, and this revolution is about nothing whatsoever.

Hiccup.

No more watching Nancy Grace. No more listening to Rush Limbaugh. No more intellectual prostitution for these pimps, no more sycophants. No more Brian Williams, no more left-wing. I've seen such smart people, so technically intelligent, rant and rave and rejoice with the voice of one Glenn Beck. No more wishing them dead, just no more paying attention.

No more subscribing to the ideas of people who are devoid of creative independence and who are no doubt inculcated with complexes of inferiority and disproportionate amounts of individuality.

No more looking back at Tommie Smith and John Carlos as black men with black gloves. I've seen these men, men like them, who just want to be heard. I hope they never put those fists down. I hope Muhammad Ali never enlists in the Army. I hope we are to be judged, the all of us, by the content of our character.

No more status quo.

Hiccup.

The principles of trivial knowledge have to be exonerated. The application of actual facts, the realization of the real, has to be maintained by the entire society.

Sociologically, a school is to be born. Reaching from the house to the neighborhood, from the neighborhood to the community, the community to the city, the city to the state, the state to the nation, and eventually, the nation to the globe.

Two schools, one educational with subtext and buildings and teachers. One generated by parents and people, neighbors and churches and programs, but especially parents:

Public School:	**Private Teaching:**
Literature	**Virtue**
History	**Compassion**
Geography	**Sympathy**
Mathematics	**Fortitude**
Science	**Self-Esteem**
Physics	**Courage**
Psychology	**Grace**
Sociology	**Humility**

And on and on. No more Feng Shui or cold consumerism; no more political or sociological divisions of urban and sub-urban. No more athletes as heroes. No more listening to the uneducated, uninformed, or unimpressed.

No more constant external projection of our own insecurities. The ignoring of the elderly, forgetting how important their wisdoms are, their lessons and sessions on the way things used to be. It is time to listen.

This revolution is about truth.

Hiccup.

Time to become like George Washington in only one way, in: 'I cannot tell a lie.' Perhaps, leaving him behind as it came to him sending a bill to the Iroquois Nation for the expenses incurred to the Army during their extermination.

Time to forget that people have created the term 'revisionist history.'

Since the beginning, we have beheld ideals, philosophy, above our actions. We have excused ourselves from our actions under the guise of personal imperfection; we have said that only God is perfect. It is time to act the way we think.

I am sure, we can realize these ideas, not only in the surreal, not only in our dreams, but in practice. We can look at each other as absolute, as final products, with the ability to overcome that finality and perpetuate better behavior. We can see it in waves and colors and it is funny, the way we have collected ourselves. Our demographics and geographic identities. None of it is all that different. The peddler, the hustler, the gangster, the valedictorian, the ivy-league cloud-white CEO's of national enterprise. They all go to war everyday, some with guns, some with business cards, some with pencil and paper, and some with nothing but the clothes on their back and an open soul. Try to see it as the same system, the same organism.

We can get better.

Hiccup.

What is it in all of us that burns so bright, that longs for such better circumstance? It is our humanity, our All.

In the fight against oppression, of any type, we cannot be spectators. We can't root for the victory or defeat of the oppressed, we have to, like Che taught me, include ourselves in the moral suffering and eventually in the fate, of the oppressed.

The subjects merely need revision. We can relearn.

It is not an outside force or political system, or government or collection of people that is oppressing *my* mind. Oppressing *our* hopes. It is our own spiritual and intellectual mal-nutrition.

As it came to slavery, apartheid, any overt racism or ethnic suppression, the one thing that every movement in every country in every history has had in common, is that at some point, without fail, information was attained by the people being held captive. They learned that they deserved better. They deserved to be and see and feel equal.

True compassion, in my mind, and in the mind of the thinkers I have sought to learn from, does not simply require of us the giving of money to the poor. Giving clothes to those who are cold; food to those who are hungry. True compassion involves fighting, in every day ways, to change the system that produces these poor.

Hiccup.

The system in this case, is our own righteous and inadequate sense of ownership and individuality.

We can hunger for knowledge, and see where it takes us.

No more fear of Socialism. A political, economic, or sociological application of Socialism is not practical, perhaps not needed or desired. But I desire an ideological application of Socialism; common effort, common production. Common shares of happiness and truly beneficial and national healthcare.

Communist views on food. The minimization of our intake of food, especially foods so high in fat content and overloaded sugar substance. Like Tupac said:

Let's change the way we eat, let's change the way we live, and let's change the way we treat each other...

None of the rhetorical concepts of charity that the right wing and left wings both spew in the senate and congress. If forgiving foreign debts from poor countries will make them, the world, and therefore us, better for it, then do it simply with the idea in mind that no matter how much money we all make, we never take it with us to the next great place. It is just money, impermanent, fiscal, hilarious. What can last is humanity acting so carelessly and compassionately...divine.

Let us treat ourselves with dignity and pragmatism. Stressing the necessities in our homes and communities of healthy behaviors. Study; eating habits; hard work; exercise; giving; crying.

Hiccup.

The importance of acknowledging and appreciating an opposing point of view. Looking at facts, not rushing to judgment. Maybe even becoming like Steve Biko, wonderful at seeing new evidence, adjusting the way we think, and even going as far as to develop the other line of thinking further than it has already been expressed.

No more rejection of moral men, on any grounds.

Steve Biko wrote poetically about the power of self-knowledge. While everyone in his country was focused on the injustices being brought upon the black people in his country by the white oppressive government, he transformed his goal to make his people aware of the injustices they were committing against themselves. By allowing and encouraging self-hate, self-distrust.

Let us keep singing.

Hiccup.

We have allowed the women in our own country, the beautiful and more beautiful and insecure, to begin truly hating their own reflections. We have allowed this to go on for decades now; we have been subversive as a culture. It took women hundreds of years to gain the right to vote, and the rest of the country, including many women themselves, about fifty years to figure out an entirely new way of subjugating them. By breaking down their physical ideas and their purest pictures of themselves.

No more 85 lb models in bikinis at the rack in the store. No more lusting at the superficial. No more ocular masturbation. Don't tell me it is evolutionary, don't tell me it is healthy for the perpetuation of the species for men to wander, to covet, and to break any hearts.

A hero, a revolutionary, is indifferent to public attention or cultural adoration.

Be revolutionary, love the women in our lives, and women, love yourselves and us back for doing so.

Hiccup.

Look not to religion for purpose or completion, look not to society for validation or congratulation. Instead, try to see the purpose of life as investigation. Try to see the expression and definition of intelligence as one's ability to grow, in all ways.

The All is not far off. The all of us appreciating here.

Include music, art, science, and love in every minute. Listen to the sounds that soothe our souls from the people who can create it much better than us.

Remember that Albert Einstein said that great spirits are always met by violent opposition from mediocre minds. Try to engage, be the great spirit, and not the mediocre mind. Remember Vietnam and the Civil Rights, Women's Suffrage and the Emancipation Proclamation. Remember each and every great event we have all been a part of.

Let us always remember the operative word in the phrase 'gay people.' It is the word people.

Hiccup.

No more talk of handing out food or giving free medical clinics in poorer areas. But recognize the power of teaching people in these places the importance and beauty of how to do it themselves, so they can feel like us. And I like them.

I come from the middle-class, the lower side of it. I hate Victorian values and uptight society. Yuppies in convertibles and rich men speaking about how they are socially conscious. A consciousness that is born of social concern and magnitude would prevent any man from claiming as such and living in a 15 million dollar home, with only a few people and a few friends.

I come from a place that requires people to put their money where their mouths are, and their hearts where their eyes are.

I want to hear no more of changing the system, of cute little stories of donation and self-congratulation, I want to see people get muddy. I want to see people, especially the people gifted with resource, revolutionize their lives, give it all away, and then do an interview with Larry King.

I want to see poor people become rich, and rich people to become rich in their humanity.

Hiccup.

We don't have to change the system. We can change the way we experience it.

I want to hear no more interviews from Hollywood or Baliwood, no more quotes of ferocity from Rodeo Drive or Manhattan, no more speeches or rhymes about the pain of the soul, without any direct action. I have no more patience or time for separation, for degradation, for insulation.

Sell that house, give up that quarter-million dollar car, and feed people while you break down the doors of every political and social facility and demand that the richest one percent start giving back ninety-nine of it.

Do that, and you will become revolutionary. New to this landscape and materialistic climate. Do it not, and just keep quiet.

Read of Patrice Lumumba and Nelson Mandela, of South America and IndoChina, and all parts of Europe. Learn about what we are, and then come back to me and spit about the land of the free and the home of the brave.

Thank the people in your life as I do:

Thank you John Legend, and the legend John Lennon. Thank you Hemingway and Gandhi, thank you Einstein and Picasso and Aristotle. Thank you Plato and Socrates. Thank you to Tracy Chapman, Alicia Keyes, and Lauryn Hill. Thank you Sam Cooke and Marvin Gaye. Billie Holliday and Etta James. Thank you Bob Marley and Kurt Cobain and Bradley Nowell. Thank you Tupac Shakur, the Notorious B.I.G., Nas, Kanye West, and especially these last ten years, Eminem. Thank you Clive Owen, Denzel Washington, Brad Pitt, Colin Farrell, Benicio Del Toro, and Ryan Gosling. Thank you Paul, George, John, and Ringo, thank you Beatles. Thank you Mya for giving them to me. Thank you Malcolm and Marcos, Che and everyone. Thank you Sarah Palin for just going away. Thank you Dave Chapelle, Richard Pryor, and George Carlin. Thank you to Russell Simmons, and to Run, for showing me what a father is. Thank you Copernicus and Galileo and Stephen Hawking, thank you Brian Greene. A special thank you to Jon Stewart and Stephen Colbert and Bill Maher, for being the humorous reason that should rule this planet. The ironic freedom of progressive thought and inclusionary jokes. Thank you JFK for trying to kill Castro, and for the nightmare Bay of Pigs. Thank you George Bush, both of you, for the Middle East. Thank you Harry Truman for never responding to the pleas of Ho Chi Minh. Thank you Howard Zinn, for the truth. Thank you all Presidents, for allowing the White House to be run by business, not personality. Money and power, instead of ethics and morality. Thank you Barack, for simply trying to change that culture. Thank you Saul Williams, the greatest poet of my day.

Thank you all for having me on my knees, listening and watching to the rhythms and schisms in our lives. For helping me notice our passion and our beauty, our frailty and our purity.

Thank you for helping me realize that in hell, I will simply need headphones.

Thank you for opening my eyes, and helping them to drip with the seething discontent of too much love.

This revolution is about sobriety. Psychological sobriety. If I may find it.

Hiccup.

(TRIAL AND ERROR)

19..

I would like to think it was *Half Nelson*. Me so tragic and brilliantly alone, trying to live halfway down, just hanging on. Music soft and hard at the same time, too smart to stop. Too slow at times, too fast too.

It felt more like *Requiem for A Dream,* a crazy ride divined by the drug-addict gods, with me left to sift. A manic, poetic mess with the left of some men bumping into each other.

But it was definitely most akin to *Intervention*. A sad and predictable plight of one more man too beaten to pretend anymore. Too weak to refuse.

Whatever, the night still has me by the throat. With time to recline and look back over the years, through the eyes of a marshmallow man, the explanations and invariable excuses seem so dramatic. All of the yelling and propagandist frowning never convinced anyone of anything. The moments I sat and looked, welled up with the ones that cared, and honestly spoke of the tortures, were real and measured. When I was really relating, I was in between the pain and the recovery.

Lately, it all sounds so blown, so out of proportion, so overgrown and so rough and distorted. But I am forced to remember how it was when I was there, it was real and thick and dark and scary and dramatic.

Out of rehab is an endless parade of red-flag dryness. I still want. When I am sober, I am not without alcohol. It is with me, I am not obsessed over it or consistently looking for it, but I am always aware of the fact that I can disappear. At times I can taste it. At times, my stomach warms randomly and I must stable myself, wondering if I took some without knowing.

When I went in to rehab I had heard of being 'dry' before. Only after did I really get it.

I haven't had a drink in almost sixty days, but I am a sponge looking for puddles. I am not sober for the love of sobriety, for the passing of normal days and rewarding experience. I am sober because I know that I will eventually have to be. I am sober because it could be a way for people to look up to me, to admire my recovery in all of its splendor. I am sober because I do not want to die, not because I sincerely want to live. This is something I just have to face.

There is definitely a recognition, a fact I am cognizant of always. If I drink, it will kill me. But...probably not right now. I am always waiting for the breaking point, with an evil knowledge that I am waiting, not just living. It is impossible to tell the ones around you, who have paid for you, who have waited themselves, that you know the nightmare has not ended. That yes there has been progress, but I still want to drink.

Even writing it thus, it sounds as though I am okay with it. It sounds like I casually observe this and say it with conviction. Though I hate it, and still just hang onto honesty.

I drive my car around some more, to work, to mundane eventualities, the car that has been through so much. I am trying to smell different smells in it, not notice the circular burns created by the slipping cigarettes of nodded-out fiends. There are dents all about the outside, on every side, reminding me of forgotten bumps and bruises I had long stopped caring about. I lost this car, I called the cops and they found it. When I met them there, the officer found a bottle of Clear Eyes on the floorboard, and handed it to me. It was over $200 worth of acid, browned from being cut with Tequila.

I have been hit by a slow-going semi on the passenger side; I have backed in to a Range Rover who I never heard from, while hitting a crack-pipe; my car has even been stomped by a rampaging pack of Metro State baseball players. I have nodded in it, smoked out of it, and slept on it.

I have trashed this little car, this vehicular vein, and it smells of me and my failures. It smells of good times too, but those are also saturated with the stench of the recent. That stink, that smell of the things that have happened lately, so by nature, are they more relevant.

My red car is the symbolic mangle of my dented life. So, soon after rehab, I go to get rid of it.

In rehab we were told that some of the things in our lives will remind us of what we were before we got better, huh, if only some. So if an opportunity arose whereby I could move on from the red suitcase of hissy-fit memories, I should do so. I should leave what I could behind. Because what keeps us comfortable in our miseries is often only familiarity.

I started injecting this tiny practice the second I got out, throwing away all of the little things around me that reminded me of how I hated. I replaced my writing pens, got a new keychain, new belt, new shoes. Same old arrangement of my pockets, so it's a sliding scale. They tried to tell us that if we couldn't take our watch off of our wrist and place it on our other wrist, and wear it there, we were in danger of relapse. We couldn't get out of old habits, we were hopeless. I hated it and didn't participate, and the foreshadowing began.

Getting a new vehicle seems backwards. Like I ran through the tape and took the picture only seconds after they fired the gun. I have done nothing to earn a new vehicle, dropped in my lap, but vocalize my yearning for new beginnings.

Sure, I have shown up to my job for a short while, I have not binged, and have answered the phone. People around me were encouraging, I was just saying how I needed to start fresh, and it did feel like time.

I get a new truck from a guy who found the vans for the company I work for, my father's company. A pick-up, I buy it. But don't speak to it honestly for a while.

Driving a car other than the one that you know your sad in…is good. The truck fills me with hope, with a four-wheel drive attitude, with a sense of invincibility. It gives me a rush driving anywhere in it for a while. It feels like power. But not the physical kind. I get to create new moments in a vehicle I call my own, that hasn't happened for a long time. I feel confident when I ride in it, a child with his new toy.

Maybe that is how it is for everyone, we sick ones just have a much more jagged edge. A lot of time was dedicated in treatment to the presentation of our sickness in a number of different ways so that we could learn from different people, at different speeds. But a constant was the incessant ringing of us having 'emotional diseases.' We were told that the alcohol is just a symptom, the drugs are just a band aid, really, we can't control our feelings. Maybe when regular people go out and buy a car they are fueled with an urge to drive around, to use, and to show and to be seen. Maybe their stomach boils up and the hairs stand straight on their arms, they shake in their shoes and hold the steering wheel tight. And half an hour later, the exhilaration is gone, but the want is still. Maybe. Maybe I just haven't been strong enough to control the urge of regular beings, maybe everyone feels the way I do and I just have been too weak to resist. How do I know?

I have an impasse. I have a new truck, I am writing, I am reading a bit, I am working, I am learning at work, I am slowly gaining a superficial trust. I have been thinking for a long time about what the truth is: Am I fully responsible? Complaining about the troublesome pursuit of a pain that I alone created? Or am I real. Was it hell? Was I a victim? Do people who are not addicted have a right to accuse me of being so selfish?

It is a mixture of both. Some of it is annoying, a broken record of same song promises, it is a very selfish condition. Even 'condition' sounds like a cop-out. But some of it is horrible, and some of us don't want it.

Mentally, my intentionally directed visions of future, my condensed, essential and sensual foresights do not include any poisonous liquid. I would be happy in those places to never see alcohol again. But my body, my ephemeral will, I can still sense their capriciousness.

But to say will is to give license to the misinformed. I can say: This condition has absolutely nothing to do with the *will power* to stop myself from using. I am the strongest person I have ever known. And most of the addicts in rehab can probably say that about the circles they are in too, for it takes an enormous amount of will power to score each and every day. It has nothing to do with strength. It has to do, purely and exclusively, like everything else in human life, with *value*. No matter how aware I am of the size and immediacy of the impending loss if I do use that substance, it still has enough quality left in it for me to take it. I am not too weak to say no, I just do not understand why I would say it. I feel ill for an indefinite period of time, no matter how long, and then I use, and very briefly, I feel calm, and balanced, and loved.

With the tickle still in me, still playing with me, I must say that I don't think I have used for the last time in my life. And instead of saying this, admitting to its possibility, I bate people I don't know very well, or couldn't be closer to, into giving me advice. Then I weigh it. Then I resent it. I take the help and make my murder.

Have I been exaggerating? Someone told me recently that he 'understands,' no one else does, but he does.

See, he remembers people saying that. That they understand. But he understands. He has had a long battle with quitting smoking. Quitting smoking cigarettes. He is someone who I have always known, and never. He is everyone that knows me, that knows I'm an addict.

I want to ask him, yell him and tell him, and a hundred others:

Have you ever smoked crack until your teeth fell out? Have you ever had someone die in your arms? Have you ever seen your best friend get shot? Have you ever had a gun in your mouth with the finger on the trigger? Have you ever been in jail, even for a night? Have you ever faced prison? Have you ever done heroin? Have you ever shoved needles in your arms? Have you ever been so high on meth you can't feel your body? Have you ever begged for death? Have you ever done things, things you can't take back? Have you ever done so much coke you can't eat for a week even after you stop? Have you ever had a complete stranger crawl to your feet in an empty house, crawl to you and beg for it to slow down?

And then he would say, "No, I have never made poor decisions like those."

I feel like this, as well as all things in life, are really just comparative tolerances generated by the worst or best of our parents that lie within us. He must have had a parent die of cigarettes, and so feels passionately about being able to quit.

Keep the stories of old and ridiculous tales of marginally tough roads, quitting cigarettes, and let the warriors travel on.

So, I can say, I know, because people try to give me the answers, that my questions are real. I don't have to feel like I am being a baby, like I am glorifying in any way how gross and large it all was. For it is serious. It is real, I have done it all, and buying new cars isn't going to take that away.

I did not expect the amount of people who "understand" to exist here, around now, but they are here. Sarcasm still saves. I thought that upon leaving treatment people would be asking me how to do it, how I learned to keep the madness away, but they already know. They know because they have also had troubles, or they had a brother who once didn't want to stop taking pills.

I guess I should just be happy that it isn't a hundred years ago, that the momentum of popular consciousness has moved towards a general sympathy, instead of violent repulse. But still so fresh, that is so hard.

I see people that I am meeting for the first time, or people that have heard of me through others, and as soon as the subject is broached I am ready to be saved. People in AA, I am happy or sorry to say, are by far the worst. All broken and trying. Out of all of the people that lean in and lower their voices, the dedicated and flamboyant followers of Bill W. are the only ones who don't ask any questions. And, the steps are the only way. The only way, and go drink until you figure that out. They actually say that to people in some of those meetings. No one told me that when I got out of rehabilitation all of the people who looked away or actively avoided would now be specialists in the field of addiction recovery. They all come and tell me, and my kindness and the fact that it catches me totally off guard every time probably implies that I am receptive. Inside I am not. Maybe I will be, but now I am not.

Of course they truly want to help, I am forced to assume, but I shamefully admit to being a stubborn old man, a man who believes in his own mind and has no time for unsolicited, sometimes condescending dictation.

I have made my decisions.

You can keep your cute little anecdotes, this isn't anything to brag about, but it isn't a life that everyone can live through either. What I have been through, what I have put myself through, I am sure, can be bared by the bravest and that is it. I have spent years now trying to decide on a language that will help my cause, my elocution must reflect a desire not to offend. I have been trying to think of ways to relate to others the power and isolation of my pull. If I sound as though I don't appreciate what you have been through, then forgive me, but I did not ask. I do not care anymore if people are offended, they may have heart, but they know nothing.

I am not talking about being disrespectful, or even dismissive. I am talking about totally ignoring every human being who presumes to understand what the cure for another may be. I don't have time for it anymore. If we can share, count me in for an indefinite amount of time; but if any person, of any age, is presumptuous enough to believe they have found my singular cure, I tune out. I am working on accepting, but still want vengeance with people who are foolish enough to challenge my intellectual dedication. I cannot wait to know what they know.

Because they may know that now I have eighty-one days sober, a sum total of less than one semester. I have had eighty-one days sober for the first time in forever, and I drive my truck. They may know that I am giving honest effort, but they don't know that another addict is hugging me from afar, and that I have already given in.

New vehicle, new insights, new treatment receipts, a new sign is in order. I wish to stand there like so many people, on the corner employing:

Please, anything helps

I will be out there soon I think, but mine will say what is true:

Please, nothing helps

We have all agreed on what is consumed with money given to the crumbling men and women who ask strangers for change. Then someone calls me on the eighty-first day. And helps me get there too. I am driving, working, starting to sleep, anticipating a functioning intestinal system, washing my lifestyle. He calls me after a brief time of sobriety of his own and tells me he is in trouble.

In any circle, predicated on the inability to separate your desires from a friend who likes the same, the response to this should be: No. Absolutely no. But I am a righteous man who knows that he is not finished, and this man gives me a way out.

They really say, in any "recovering" circle, that it is okay to pick up another addict, if they haven't been using. They say that you can run, you can strap yourself to a missile if you like, when your friend calls and needs help. And…is sober. But if there is a person on the other end of the line who wants help, but has the same weaknesses as the slough who answers, everyone should run. Do not be so presumptuous as to believe that it can work any way other than that which you have already experienced a thousand times over. Your friend is not like the others either, and he has what is worth having.

Any addict who tells you he is fine, he is just going to help a friend who is using, be sure to tell him goodbye. I drove to him to use, not to help.

He called me, and I used him. I am using him because I don't have the courage to go and take a drink by myself. If alcohol was different now than when I went in to treatment, I better find out. I know, and I knew moments after leaving treatment that I still *wanted* to drink, but didn't know positively that I would. And I didn't want to want it any more. But now I know.

I go to pick him up, and halfway there I relapse. I relapsed the second I said to myself, 'I am going to drink today.' It isn't important that I don't drink for another hour. I was hammered before any swallowing.

I finally get him from where he is, a bar with mugs and taps. I pick him up in my new truck, get him in, and head for my apartment, where he is welcome to stay.

He has his face down as we ride towards my house. He is shuffling his shoulders the way we do, bobbling his head. He is swaying and mumbling, and I want it. I stop and barely acknowledge to him that I am going in to the liquor store.

As I get back on the highway I open a bottle of vodka. I smell the vodka. I contract and wince and cough and come. I open the Sprite, put the vodka to my mouth and then wash down the gulp with some soda. I talk to my friend for a bit, about hate, about sobriety, and about futility. I talk to him and we coax each other to dream a little, to dream about lives which don't involve any mind-altering substances. I speak casually, feeling freer than I have in about three months.

Just down the street from my house I make the call. My friend doesn't want to do coke, and I laugh. I tell him, "I'm sorry."

The first hit of the coke and I am flying. This moment has been coming since the day I committed to go to rehab, but I hoped that it never would. I am terribly sad, and finally comfortable again. I make three huge lines for myself, and do them. It feels like I did it the day before. Like I never stopped. The sounds, the taps, the cuts, the eventual inhale. The lash that tilts you back and dramatically rushes to numb your gums. The burst when the first one hits, it has been a while. When I clear all three lines I lean back and rub my mouth with my finger. My eyes close and then I take a huge drink of vodka. I try to finish my pint, just about fifty minutes and $60 worth of coke after I bought it. I talk to him, my friend who is me, I swig and snort, and hours in finally catch what has happened. It was just too fast. I am ashamed, the universe is now contracting, collapsing, everyone is ashamed, I get more and more. I happen to be here.

We are always saying that. It just happened, or I don't know. Or the day was just right, or my sister upset me, or the jerks at the DMV, or my team just can't win, or I hate my mother, or any number of transparent excuses to replace the obvious: I love being drunk, or: I am not yet exhausted of it. Or, against boredom even the gods fight in vain. I love listening to music after one giant bottle of Everclear and three grams of cloud inside a half hour. I love the feeling of not feeling. For a time.

Knowing that I have a genetic addiction to alcohol, that in me and in "drug-addicts" is either a retarded electron or a corrupted frequency or a weak strong nuclear bond, the smart thing for me to do, to have done, would have been to stop the second I noticed. Never another drink, never another ride down that dangerous river. The first time I got drunk, and absolutely loved it, I should have run for the hills. Some people are able to do so, recognize that they are going to be addicted, and stop. Some people are not addicted physiologically, they are psychologically addicted. They are crazy and pained and love losing the way they feel. Some hate to drink, but *are* too physically addicted to decline their medicine. Some have it in them, and they also just love to drink for all of the reasons that none of us are supposed to. That is my theory, and I am both.

Some people think that they had a huge problem, like my father, but knew it was getting bad, and that they 'overcame' addiction by just throwing away the cocaine. Some are delusional, and all that means if you pre-emptively threw it away is that you are not addicted.

I believe it is in my blood, I am bio-chemically changed the instant I use. I am severely clinically addicted, *and* I love it. I love to snort, I love to drink, I love to be high. I love when my eyes are dropped and everything I say sounds so romantic.

But I also am not comparable to almost any other addict I have ever met. There is an element of illness in my sickness, a physical, digressive, isolated, *disease*. I feel so sick – so devoid of joy, of balance, of foresight, of physical senses. So achy, nauseas, stuffed, robust, heavy, full, and empty.

This time is no different, no huge canyons to cross because of treatment. It took me no effort to decide, nothing had changed, nothing has changed. Maybe it has, but it has changed on the back end of the bender. The first second I heard his voice, I knew I was there. Everyone begins calling us the next day, it is a Friday, there are marginal expectations.

But we drink, he sleeps mostly, he dozes and wakes and sips and sleeps. I do. I spend hundreds on coke, plenty on booze, I am and was right where I thought. I do not want to be a drunk anymore, but I still want to get drunk.

Still, even now, the amount which I can consume, is astonishing. Without exaggeration, the amount I consume on an average bender would kill over 75% of human beings who would venture, randomly, to attempt to match it. Two, one point seven-five liters of alcohol, and six teeners of blow, in thirty six hours. It is not pride, but shock.

I didn't even get three months, and the withdrawals are horrible. Us explaining to everyone how and why, going to post-rehab support groups with people who have attended the same center, telling the ones we love. Looking at my people again, my family, and my Mya, and telling them that I have been gone again.

* * *

I will not start off with any Dickens. Nothing like that.

Shortly after my first, was my second. Then my third, and eventually something fun.

Somewhere in the four times that I relapsed after seeking, sprinting for help and taking only some of it in, I was a trailer-park superstar.

I do not remember when exactly it was, at least the date or between or part of which episode, I really have no way of knowing. I build up now, thinking about it. I can't run exactly at it, grabbing my mother by the back of the head and slamming her head into a wall. I just can't really mention it right away, I must think hypothetically around it.

What if I had never picked up a drink? What if, you know, this and that and I could have been and how is it wrong and all of that...but what if? It is not the apocalypse, no gestating catastrophe, but it stings. It stings and stinks and rings of things too much to bare.

Friday night there were bugs on the floor. The house party was sloppy. It was an uncomfortable crowd of people for me. Nothing outright, nothing ominous or blatantly threatening or anything, though the ceiling felt an inch from the top of my head. The cigarette smoke played right by me and spilling beer was in the room. Just uncomfortable, just dingy.

Just enough to totally reason: I don't have to leave, I can just drink a little. I *can* be comfortable, I can't wait for the warmth. Knowing there was no shot, no chance at immediate redemption, no illusory notions of typical behavior, I still know and knew and will that

that night I was just going to have a couple. Just like the thousands of nights that I had totally, shamelessly, lied to get what I wanted. Lied to me briefly, to anyone else that would listen, lied unapologetically and still feel curiously proud of always sticking tough with tough and sticky. I was going to drink, I was so so sorry, but still nothing was more important. This time, at this anxiety party, it was still and predictable and I went home drunk.

Somewhere later this thing happened, this grabbing and slamming thing. This morbid creation of people who are related getting too old to use together in any way without incident.

I remember she came to help, to caress her boy and soften his expression. Her lucid memories of my semi-homelessness, her nauseatingly, authentically guilty conscience, brought her up after I was supposed to have learned, but was all the worse. Maybe the worst I have been.

She did help for a while, but I knew I could be mean. I was horribly irritable and truly desperately wanted more cocaine. She stood me up naked in the shower and helped me let water wash over me. I soaped and died, and ended up falling asleep on the couch I believe. It blurs together forever and cycles and storms in patterns of weather. It is horrible to not remember, I have thought that enough, but the mood changed on waking up.

In my state, warped with squints, she was aggressive, angry somehow, and I thought how dare she, how dare anyone not be unlimitedly compassionate. This anger, this familiar undertone of far too much conviction came to me, as it does soberly sometimes in very light and honest ways.

But the booze had changed. I laugh and think of how I thought I didn't think it could happen. I had changed, actually. But it was mad after treatment. I was mad, I scowled and occasionally caught sight of my reflection at times, and later cried so hard at how hard I tried not to become so irrationally angry and truly mean, only to see me at many unfortunate times. I wasn't a happy person, people, and pitifully, myself, thought like so many others who make such simple, easy, and gratifying self-assurances, that going to an official rehabilitation center would solve or greatly reduce so much of the dramatic.

She said something about leaving in some threatening way, I told her fine, get out. I got up, groggy and tired and violently defensive. I still think so poorly of those times. It is self-pity, and sadness for humanity, and anger at myself, and anger at whoever is involved for letting someone "so drunk" get them so angry, and a feeling of being so subserviently worthless, defeated and so failed at keeping said promises. Unbelievable, what looking someone in the eye, shaking their hand, and telling them so biblically that they can give you what is oh so sacred, their deaf and dumb belief in what has become your once-again wavering trustworthiness.

She shouldn't have trusted me before that, and I got up off the couch and walked in a way that represented no restraint or respect and began pulling her arm, trying to get her to the front door. She said no, and we ended up in the kitchen. All the strength left in my skinny arms, my stupid, tiring weak frame and bloated stomach, again, couldn't calmly or even at all, convince my mother to ignore my violence and talk. So we kept on for a second, I don't remember just before it but I grabbed the back of her head and slammed the front of it into the wall right by my refrigerator.

Rehab wasn't gone, a figment or as far away as me, but here it was not. The notions of peaceful, cooperative, progressive reasoning with others was reduced to its most primitive form.

Quick to be angry, disproportionate amounts of energy directed at the person, no tactic for calming or taking a break, drunk, mean, no phone call, no chance at going back, no real help for the hopelessness of once again. Look what has happened even after the effort, I feel not good. Look what I am doing, this is sadder than before. What rehab finalized was the realization that the time for bandanas on my head and big chains or whatever little way I had adapted was over.

I didn't hit her head solidly, with the force I would have with a man, or with the intent of injuring. But how…how does one, as rhetorically philosophical as possible, look at himself after grabbing his own mother in such a way. No matter what she had done or said, she is the reason I am.

How could I have done that? Possessed or not. The chemicals replace the molecules that make up your mind, and you still sound like you are excusing yourself any time you refer to yourself in the third person in such an event. I did this. I am here to deal with doing that.

The time of people being around occasionally, and those not so closely involved still making jokes at how they drink too much too, have ceased. Somberly, I told I went to get help, and I failed within three months. I don't think I should be considering suicide, but I feel not good Mya, this is not triumphant. Everyone who knows me is truly sad for me, searing pain in the eyes of people who barely know me, for someone they partially believe will make it. I felt lighter before, just out, but heaviness with the frustration of the old resurfacing has me in deep, barely spared.

* * *

What is it in us, that we can fill our hearts with such progress, but only give to the world our frightening failures?

When I first heard her voice in jail I was furious, madder than she. I was going through such horrible withdrawals in a cell with a dominant Mexican, someone who did not much like me. I was terrified and totally ready and not scared at all. Jail is empty, no matter how many people they cram into it. But your cell seems full, packed with aggressive personality, you have to be ready for anything really, and I was hallucinating.

It was a couple weeks since I was at the bug party, the house with the floor with the people. My friend's house. I love my friend with all of my heart, he is like a brother, a soldier holding his musket standing behind me. Less violent, but never did he ever leave me behind. When I was gone, his phone calls never stopped either. I could hear in his voice, the strange idea that his friend may be dead, and his house should have been as comfortable as any. But since I left treatment and waved goodbye to the me satisfied with such an indecent lifestyle, I have had coronary anxiety.

Nervous all the time, my friend who makes me feel safe couldn't protect me from his house, and I got hammered like always. Soon after I did sophisticated amounts of cocaine.

Then I did a lot more cocaine. And drank a lot of beer.

Then it was a Sunday, and I drank nineteen beers, at 3.2%.

I wrote all of this down, for some inconceivable reason. Mostly, I can't even sit up on the couch when I am drinking without speed. But I wrote down that after that I had two pints each day, two coke sacks each, two broken meals each, two too much incidents, crawling on the bathroom floor.

Then it was a Wednesday - I squeezed in two pints. I looked around at my living room: My couch was given to me by an old roommate, those strange old patterns they burdened us with in the 70's and 80's, dingy a bit, stains of my insides. I had an old entertainment center, I didn't like it. A particle board desk, an old roller-chair from high school with the hard plastic backs. A bedroom with merely a bed and a dresser. It was so easy to surrender in this particular apartment, so reminded of my radical extremes.

Signs were everywhere of me hanging on, smells.

The inability to remember details leading to significant events is sometimes advantageous, but no matter what, I usually have to remember the biggest of all of the negativities. After hitting my mother, forgetting my father.

She left at some point whenever, and I was on my couch, looking to my right at my sister and her boyfriend. Days after I restarted and repudiated. I thought of how good it would feel to be sober, I felt their smiles, and the door opened directly in front of me. I had been drinking for days, weeks, decades, saying whatever to whomever, and the police and paramedics walked into my apartment.

At first: Brief paralyzation. Then rage. I look at my sister and yell at her, "You did this." Once, I told her that no matter what, no matter how many screams I screeched out, do not call an ambulance. Do not, do not, call the cops.

So she totally ignored me, the ungrateful brat. The selfish girl called the police because I kept calling her, making no sense, incoherent, babbling about pain and an ambulance and suicide.

The paramedic was female, I can't remember her name but I remember her kneeling in front of me. She was kind, she asked me if I was okay. I was physically okay, I was going to make it I'm pretty sure, but I was mad. That anger that comes from nowhere, and is projected everywhere?

The officer who accompanied everyone was standing very close to me the whole time. Right above me, imposing his ferocious and intimidating will, he kept alert. I was sitting on the couch sort of reasoning whether to allow the woman to run her tests, but I became panicked. I just wanted a minute, I just wanted to collect myself, but I imagine it didn't come across as a very passive action. I stood up quickly and the officer grabbed my arm, of course, as hard as his empty little hand could, and I shot something verbal at him. This was a mess, I'm sure, not nearly as coherent or simple as I am thinking it now.

I wrenched my arm from his hand. I have never deliberately, disrespectfully, disobeyed a police officer. I have demanded, without warrant in their eyes, that I be treated proportionately. I realize that I am being difficult, I am not being violent, I am not cursing, I am

Gandhi. I am practicing non-violent non-cooperation. I don't like the force that police use with anyone, but recognize that most do so because they have had to use it with someone.

In any case, he grabbed me again, and said, "You want to go to jail?," in that pathetically veiled attempt at wielding any meaningful power. I told him yes, and I didn't wait for him, I left my apartment and walked straight down to his car with him trying to keep pace behind me. I was mad.

On the way in to jail I asked him two things: Can I have a cigarette? Hell no, and he picked up the pace, now with me handcuffed, I struggled to keep up. And then: What am I being arrested for? He told me: for resisting arrest.

I cannot believe that I remember any of it. But it is there, little pictures and videos, clips of a life lived between dying.

The problem with police is that they are human beings as well. They are as imperfect and incomplete in all those areas like everyone else, but while they are developing these areas of their personalities they are incrementally in total control of someone else's freedom. Their livelihood.

I am reminded of Steve Biko, explaining his conflict with authority. He said that in the end, if he were treated with decency, with the expressed and cautious kindness that police officers can be capable of, he was bound to be effected by their humanity. He would respond honestly, helpfully, he would see them as he sees himself. The second, the very moment the police began getting aggressive physically, or abusive verbally, they became inhuman to him. He responded like an animal because he felt like an animal. He was being caged and pushed and demanded, and with the thoughts of people who are not strong enough to do so for themselves, or thoughts of the dignity and respect he must demand for himself and especially for his family, he would respond in kind to the way he was being treated. He would defend himself to the death, because death was the most natural and unchanging part of life, the time which you go and the courage it takes to deal with it, were the only things left for him to control. He was not going to give his life, they must take it. And they did. And for reasons as yet undiscovered, I take this and a million other historical injustices personally, and I believe in Einstein: Blind faith in authority is the enemy of truth.

The first part of jail is a blur, I was drunk and withdrawing and high. I was crying in booking, crying quietly in the corner about the fact that going to jail had somewhere become acceptable in my life. Crying because I was thinking of dying. The police in booking went to move me, with Biko on my mind, I stood strong. I was not being disobedient or combative, but I was going to go under my own strength, without being pulled or tugged or pushed or shoved. They disagreed.

They jammed me and slammed me, cracking my forehead on the concrete wall. I did not flail or whine, I stood up. They told me they were not going to take any resisting, I turned straight at them, with any of the energy I had left un-soaked by alcohol, and calmly said that I did not wish to resist, I just wanted to be treated with respect. And they did. And I was free to look around, to begin becoming sober, in jail, again.

I got into holding, straight away, I was still too drunk and one of the kinder guards took me in to a giant room with cells, and took me to a cell and ordered the large Mexican man to get up and sleep on the top bunk. He was none too happy with me for that. But I finally passed out, got some sleep, re-ordered my interaction.

The picture on my badge was one of me without any joy, it is one I have never seen but can imagine that my loved ones have for years. I look empty in some way, no rage, no fear, no joy, no worry, catatonia. That isn't me, I am loud. My name does not include any numbers in its spelling.

So the movie goes. I sit ironically on the outlying rocks by the beach, or in jail, the tide coming in, hair tousling in the wind, when a small, deliberate smile hits my face like I have something figured out. In the middle of chaos, people, and card-playing, and arguing, I soak in my surroundings. I am on no real, healthy sleep, they will give me no medicine, and there is no TV, no newspapers, no magazines, no pencils, no paper, no nothing while you wait 72 hours for general population. I am forced, and at some point, resigned, to think more purely, more objectively, and just be. Just sit, in this clean dirty place, and think of everything outside it.

For someone like me, the most glaring and painful absence in jail is the absence of art. There are creative people in gen-pop, some incredibly wasteful artists, but none of them can put art on the walls, none of them have the motivation to write poetry, at times the radio can be illusively satisfying, but I can't watch or see or hear what is my favorite. And that is painful.

I take in the silence, the murmuring heroes.

It is not being able to indulge a particular taste that is incredibly pure, it is missing a part of yourself. In jail, not prison, but county jail, if you want to stay out of trouble, you can. But nothing changes the fact that time, with absolutely no distractions, moves at a strangely depressing pace. It is funny to want to be getting older faster.

Thus these men, guilty or innocent, who sometimes are inclined to come to this place for half of a lifetime off and on, spend their days speaking of sports or religion, or mostly talking lightly about what got them there again. They all talk, I listen and twist with the creature in me, feeling outside of the I, they speak of bad raps and unfair pursuits, of being deceived by those they love and of the unnecessary and highly funded, conspiratorial case against them. I watch them patiently, and feel curiously out of place in jail for the first time. I always thought of 'rights of passage' to manhood, and 'I did my time,' and now I think: I am wasting away in my life, witness to the hanging of my own self-respect. I cry again, don't care who sees, don't care who knows, I cry because I am sorry for doing so many horrible things to myself. To me.

I have ended up so many times without any philosophical, historical, sociological, physical, or moral identity. Nothing has mattered more, and I have damaged nothing greater. I have become anonymous, with no voice, and no real place in society. Or, realistically, in no big part of my lover's life. No knowledge of self. No time spent with family, no dedication to anything, but a temporary fix for an annoyingly long temporary feeling, that ends up lasting until I am liver failure. Or heart failure. Or kidney failure. Or involuntary manslaughter, or a deadbeat dad. Or in prison for the most beautiful times of my life.

I look at the concrete, the brick, the lack of any individuality, the looks, the faces, the minimalist windows, the steel as accent, the infinite amounts of the same exact room. I watch the guards interact with the inmates, and the inmates with each other. And I finally recognize, thoroughly, that it doesn't need to sound elitist or arrogant. Only practical: Me and my skill set, and my fluctuatingly pure soul, do not belong here.

Is there a type? Yeah, the man who is in and out, depriving his wife or family of his presence, or a child player, the effect is the cause and the cause the effect and round and round. But not me. I am genuinely nice. I am tougher than anyone I know. I am smarter than anyone I know. It is ok for me to believe, to say these things to myself sometimes, to keep these little things to myself, as I let them lead me to places that deserve my presence.

I see, plain as day. In here: I am free. Free: I have been a prisoner for longer than not. I am the protagonist of the ironic New York play, liberated in jail. Free of the desire, of the need. I am not withdrawing as hard, but crying just so. In jail there is no flashing sign, there is no possibility, there is no unknown. If you respect people and stay out of their way, and mind your own business, there is a level of comfort in jail that comes from the sober and infrequent times that you can count of you having no chance of getting inebriated. It is like rehab, but for me, better.

I shamefully ask for forgiveness, but I say that with enough time to think, enough time to remember, listening to myself has been the best therapy for which I could have ever asked. Always. Growing up the way I did brings benefits. I know myself, I speak to myself and listen to myself and am at times no more content than when alone. Usually not here, but. There is no chance at losing myself in jail, no chance of cutting or threatening suicide, of seeing the look on Mya's face, there is no chance at me getting coke and walking painfully about my apartment for over forty-eight hours. There is no chance at people truly feeling sorry for me, they can't see me. I can not handle, and wish to refuse to accept the necessity of, the pain in their faces. In here, I can't harm anyone. I am totally and have been totally fed up with looking at people and seeing pity. Or hurt.

In the wonder, the almost arbitrary direction and content of what we are capable of thinking sometimes, the hilarious unknown, I get to an idea I have heard for years, heard through treatment, heard as uniquely successful. The idea that achievement comes through submissiveness. Through the realization of powerlessness, through certain recognitions. This is how I have been living. Maybe I have interpreted it incorrectly, but it has caused me to be timid, a bit indecisive. Whether or not I was practicing an incorrect application or an incoherent concept is not important. I was truly trying.

What I have realized is that whatever, without being disrespectful, I was practicing, as it was taught to me, for my case, I completely disagree with. I have found new evidence of good results and power. I say in certain cases, they are wrong.

I know absolutely everything.

The idea of achievement is in effort. I need not chips, or key-chains, or coffee mugs. I need to be happy with the idea that whatever in life it is, whatever, I must believe that my best will be good enough, or if not, I will be good enough to live with my best.

I need to take back, take charge.

I need to know, not think, know, that one day I'm going to die.

The idea of powerlessness, of giving over to someone or something else, is backwards to me. I sit in jail, glad to have been here, to have told the judge I wanted to stay as he decently tried to tell me that the state had no case, and that I could get out of jail immediately. I sit here and realize that the power of owning my own life and making my own decisions, as long as they are good, being proud, being full, is mine. It is the timidity, the powerlessness, the fear of judgment, the questions, the giving over, that keeps me sick. I need to stand proud, to fail with dignity, to forget quickly, to be stronger than the pity.

I need to make myself stronger, to believe in my good ideas, to forget the minorly insulting platitudes of people with general advice for specific problems. To forgive them immediately, even if arrogantly, and move on to what I was onto already. I need to be the power, the will, the direction of my day and of my way and of how I get through both. I have been wrong. Weaker than necessary, I think. Too quick to allow the words of others to hurt or cause defense, when I could have just said, honestly, "Thank you." And thought on my own about what they may have said, and what I think about that. I have been violently defensive, and become angry with people often and disproportionately, and then have gone on to take their advice anyway. It is nonsense.

With the years of irritatingly constant necessities of probation, the urine tests, the ignition interlock, the trips in and out of jail, the DUI's, the lawyers, the judges, the DMV required meetings, and the strip searches in Weld County, I have grown tired of being docile. I have grown tired of strangers and strange things keeping me wet.

I am still tired of seeing the unjust cops, and the ones who are kind, who are still there to arrest me. I am tired of the cage, literal and figurative. I am tired of the prisons in which I have kept myself.

Because at first, you think simple things: At least I don't have a real drinking problem. Then your scales begin perpetually changing. I looked around my life after that, and I thought: At least I haven't gotten a DUI or anything. At least there isn't the garbling sirens screeching my ears, I haven't gotten into real trouble. Then there is more digression, more reductionist minimalism. At least I haven't gotten really into drugs, because my jail sentence was short but poignant, powerful and brief. At least for me, the order doesn't matter, the person doesn't matter, the tale is pretentious of every rock-bottom knock-out. Then I thought: I may be a drug addict, but at least I am not alone, at least that guy will pass the light bulb. At least, even if I can't stop drinking, I can't stop pissing for my P.O., I can still use drugs. The drugs, the ones I finally picked my face from and stayed up for days on, at least I still had a reputation and some sort of resource structure. At least I haven't been to prison. At least I haven't seen someone die. At least I haven't had seizures or gone under. It all happens. At least, at least. At least I am not dead.

We all lose everything, we all addicts, we beautiful striving addicts and non, but we addicts lose everything tangible. Everything. In the end, we all say, with a sense of resignation and melancholy, with memories of everything else we have lost: At least I have not lost my life.

We are all from the hood, childhood, adulthood, parenthood, but it's our unique ability to fit into our neighborhood that keeps us going. Others. And when they are gone, we either hold on to freedom or health.

I sit in jail and can no longer count on freedom for any amount of time. And now I think that I must give myself over to a higher power. I can't do anything for myself, what was all that. I have to shrink down, and back away. I have to let all other people in my life become God.

I have lost everything external, everything but my body that can be possessed.

I have a profound moment, seeing, clearly. Seeing that I am coming to feel as though I am a punctuation mark, right at home, with the other lazy little dots, at the end of a sentence.

*   *   *

I play traffic like the accordion it is, in pastel backgrounds sometimes, coming North along the front range, listening to the music.

Ten months later, out of jail, ten months out of my head, ten months of working and being bailed out in oh so many areas, ten months later...

Back to work for my Father, he owns a Temperature Controls Contracting company. We are only licensed to work with low voltage.

So I have learned about pressure switches, about line and load voltages, about cooling and evaporative coils, about condensers, about unit controllers, about fan speeds, about signal generators, about dampers and their associated motors, about air and heat exhaust, about power transformers, about wattage and voltage and amperage, about contactors and relays and HOA switches, about demand load limiting, about electrical flow and its curious direction and properties, about rooftop units and unit heaters and furnaces and air conditioners, about duct pressure, about smoke alarms, about duct detectors, about sump pumps, about water pumps and pressure taps and boilers and cooling towers and basements and mechanical rooms and crawl-spaces and people…and Xanax, and low-level liver enzymes, and the world with the help we live in.

Go to get more help, and I am paraded in front of protestors with signs that read: You are diseased. With: Social Anxiety Disorder, copious amounts of undue stress. Depression, not the bummers, a clinical deficiency in Serotonin. A corrupted rewards and punishments center. Bad circulation. High cholesterol, weighing 145 lbs at times, skinny from using. Maybe bi-polar disorder. A touch of Manic Depression, unique in it's grip, where I need a hole to hide in. Paranoia. Absolute insomnia. Obsessive-compulsive disorder. Psychology and psychiatry. I push on.

I am learning and wearing cover-alls, I am listening to my headphones all day. I am regulating my intake, of whatever. Ten months after being locked up and locked in, I am in Aspen, CO. I am working in a new hotel that the previous contractor botched, they were the professional equivalent of my personal disorganization. Good souls, good intentions, but huge intellectual deficiencies. Huge gaps in supposedly finished work.

I get angry at people, still, with no real real reason. My temper, which has never seemed to strangle me so, gets me in trouble so many times. I say the wrong thing to the wrong person in the wrong professional position. People upset me, if they question my work, the nature of its functionality, they have wronged me in some way philosophically. They have crossed a personal boundary and I still know people with guns and no self-worth.

I feel like a fool each day. This beautiful place, this mass of snow and property, with tuxedos and skin-tight pants inside fur-covered boots walking by, rich, snowy brick-laden streets. Expensive hotels with massive fireplaces and cloud-white valets. Ask me something one day, when I feel like me, when my eyes aren't crossed, when I haven't over-indulged in too much Coffee, then too much Xanax, and surrounded by such natural inspiration, and I will say *this*. Ask me something one other day, when I am furious with the waste of the well-off, when I am in it deep, frowning for foxholes, and I may give you a completely reasonable response to a completely reasonable question, but I guarantee you, it will be *that*. So when am I authentic? When is what I think actually me? The homunculus assessor behind the eyeballs? I know not.

All I know is that I am trying to help myself with Celexa, with small-dose anxiety pills, with hard work in a majestic monopoly.

I try to be honest and humble and modest and mumble. But being away from the big city hasn't quieted its pull altogether. I got here with a breeze, I feel like I had a break. Money is in my bank account, responsible with responsibilities. But the snake slithers its return.

You can not explain it, only maintain it. Things were so easy for so long, but things turn without concrete incident. I have always been honest, but all of a sudden: I feel like John Nash, always asking: Have I just bridged some level of honesty that borders on stupidity? Always with the, "I am Jay, and I am a drug addict and an alcoholic." Then the recognition that the man I am speaking with simply asked me, "paper or plastic?" Things spiral confusing.

Ten months went by like ten minutes, now what? I feel awful.

In fact work goes briefly well, and I well-up, told I am getting a raise. I drink Nyquil because I panic. Wrongfully accused, I accept the rewards of doing things right for just a few months.

The beautiful place where the rich save the universe offers only temporary, unsatisfying consolation. Mya is miles away, back in Denver. I am lonely, and four months in to the project, I go back down to her and get upset. We had broken up, verbally. We had been non-committal, we should see other people for a while, because for a while things haven't gone so well. But that is no excuse, Jay knew Mya still loved him.

A 19-year old girl named Peru came to Aspen, and I think she is beautiful. Then she speaks, and I think she is smart. And I fall superficially, lonely, and want such company. A couple weeks in with all of the pressure, I get drunk.

At home, for years now, Mya could have filed Missing Persons Reports. Disappearing for days and weeks - and I put Peru through something violent and familiar. I drink and I go out and I come back to the hotel I am staying in, the hotel I am working at, and I go to the bathroom. I get up off the toilet, too drunk to stand and urinate, and I fall back to crack my head, getting nine staples and MRI's and chest CT's. And mountains of hate and justified jealousy from my love Mya so far away. A taste. Nothing bigger than that for this young girl I justified myself for dating, and she just about walked away.

Mya. Mya Mya Mya.

The hotel at which I have been working forces me to leave after that, because after that, I get back from the hospital and drink steadily, the spinning recently, and won't vacate a room reserved for out of town money. I do not know.

I head back to town, back to familiarity, back to the streets and smells and defeats and swells. Back to Denver, dumped by High Society.

I head back with nowhere to live, my stuff at a friends house, exiled from Mya's house after I told her of Peru.

Sometimes I fight because I have to. Sometimes because I know I'm supposed to, sometimes because I want to. Sometimes…it is compulsory. Reflexive. Sometimes I am strongest when I am the sickest, and on the good days that end the movies, sometimes, I feel the wickedest. I feel sick, but I have my pills and my truck, and I rent a town home.

My job is somehow saved, my father, in this sense, is Superman.

Sometimes…now, I know it was a mistake. My sister moved in with me, and as much as we both have the same smile, the same soul, the same goal, we can be poison for each other. Everything too fast, from Aspen to barely employed.

We move in to the town home, and we are only concerned with rent.

You walk in the front door, and there is a landing immediately to your right, six inches off the fake-wood particle floor. Then up the stairs from the landing is a mezzanine, where you turn left and walk about fifteen feet to the two bedrooms, they look normal and have us feeling normal. Above your head as your walking is the vaulted ceiling, hanging over the entire little house. To your right as you march, down below, is the living room. A fireplace in the far corner from the waterfall walkway, down twenty feet, opposes the kitchen;

open with much too much counter space. There is a basement, a dungeon, a simple little laundry room with enough square footage to let thirty homeless men rest. The entire home is like one big room, which is important when we fall. We need separation, some out of sight out of mind time; but none is there.

Two months in, the record is broken again. She starts first, but the order is of no importance. I was bringing her medicine, against no uncommon sense. Trying to get her to slow down, unconcerned with how the first drink haunted. After so many days, the pull is too strong. The pain is too evident; I see the withdrawal and the pupils and the neurological mis-firings, I see the sadness and rambling and childhood monologues, and I take.

We relapse together, in perfect harmony, shutting out the world, counting pennies and begging each other to walk to the liquor store. It is so nice to have someone in it with me, and so horrible. But the alcohol is poison, and with enough time, it is also the antidote.

The first hundred times, it must have been doubly sad, doubly hard for the people who watched us double our trouble. After a while, they must have been hoping for two calls simultaneously, one person reporting the passing and painful release of two wrenching souls. I don't know…I don't know, I have brought that up to people. Asking people, telling them, "You must be so ashamed of me. I am causing you so much pain, it would probably be better if I were gone. Peaceful." Believing that, I am convinced I am wrong. Genuinely, sincerely, incredibly angrily, the response has been: Absolutely not.

Sometimes when I am sitting there bubbling from the nervousness, shockwaves from my brain, dirtied and damned and done and ugly, I feel a strength that pulses with my pulse, that hurts with my hurt, when I remember the look in the eyes when I mentioned this, and I push on.

We try to get it together, together.

I am working for my gracious Father still after it all, after missing two weeks. My sister is trying to get back to work, trying to not burn bridges. I am bringing in money. After the relapse, not answering the phone, leaving the other members of the company guessing at the state and condition and progression of my job sites, I have to beg. I have to go to the office and cry in front of everyone, tell them once again the beaten and weakened man has given in and puked all over. My Father is the boss, they have no choice.

Weeks before one episode he had said, "you are always chasing that first high, and you never will get back there." If he only knew how insightful that is. If he only knew that rehabs everywhere and everyone addicted knows that, he would know that that was the day I finally understood: He kind of understands.

I don't understand how he understands, I see I don't get fatherhood, and I am lucky over the years to have not been a father accidentally. Because this part of the hood, the life, I don't get yet.

The people at work don't really accept it, but he does and I am back at my job. I am working for months, months filled with too many ups and downs. Ups and downs never known, sober and dry and whatever.

I had built this mountain of hate for myself, incomprehensible, an anger that I intellectually have been acknowledging for some time, but emotionally had held for just and only me. It starts liquidating my job-sites, snapping at people I am in no position to snap at again. Yelling at bosses in hard-hats with hammers and hair. Getting myself in trouble. When my bosses, when my Father, when Mya, when I, bring it up, I spray venom again. Again and again, imbalanced and embarrassed and endangering. I do not care what I say to who, and screw you too.

I may well write one paragraph, and call that a book. It is the same over and over.

Living in this nice little home with my beloved little sister, my diet is mush. My sleeping habits aren't habits at all; they are both induced and forced and need specific recovery. When I initially relapsed in this apartment, me and my little sister, for the first time since my addiction began, my father actually showed up. He just showed up and helped.

He didn't care how he sounded to anyone. He didn't care about business meetings or ballgames anymore, he didn't care how many uncaught fish there were in the
Colorado river. All he cared about was me; just me and my impending doom or happiness, just the lonely me. I could see in his face when he showed up that he meant it. All I could see in his face was that he loved me, and he didn't want me to die. He was racked, and he didn't give me a speech…he wasn't telling me this time, he was asking me. He cleaned up my new house, unimaginable amounts of vomit in three different sinks, through the stench of an alcoholic's Vietnam.

He gave me back my house, gave me back my cleanliness, literally, for the first time in this strange place with me and her. He had never done that before. It must be bad around here.

He told me about eating right too, but I didn't listen. Now I am struggling again, with him begging me to get more help. But...I have seen enough and heard enough help.

I have heard these stories lately, after I ask, under the guise of recovery and reconciliation: Out of time and out of my mind, I begged my friend to leave her son, to leave him lay in his beautiful little bed with his cranky little eyes, and drive me to get heroin. I have heard these stories lately about myself, and they are driving me crazy. Things are fast again. I work and work and work and play, but never recover, never a day.

We both make it about five months, and my mother suddenly becomes homeless. Victimized by her own alcoholic sick, victimized by her alcoholic man, victimized by her own pitiful sense of victimization. So we take her in, she stays with us temporarily. The details of the months and the work and the sites slip me, they slip my mind, they are not worth holding. She moves in, and we three begin.

It starts with one simple thing: Someone has OxyContin. Someone we know, someone with my sister trying to work and my mom staying home under the pretense of looking for a job, has some serious pills. I knew of heroin before, but not of these.

I call him myself, because I have the money, and I am the drug addict.

It starts with 15 mg of OxyContin, and 50 mg Morphine pills. It starts with two or three more. It starts possessing me, it starts with me nodding out at traffic lights. It starts with me being much more calm, not snapping at people, not being able to see any black in my eye. No pupil at all. The blue consumes it, the beautiful blue and yellow like a circular river on a back-dropped sky. It starts with my eyelids being lower than ever. It starts with marginal functionality, re-up infrequency.

The barbiturate is the vascular gift from heaven. I am so relaxed and warm, so ecstatic and erotic.

The 30 and 40 mg Oxy pills have to come. The morphine disappears and I was done with them anyway. Over the period of a month, it starts being all that I am. I start taking over 90 mg of Oxy a day. Then 120. Still showing up to work. It starts with me pretending that I haven't become a different kind of fiend. I just plead and plea and talk of my ignorance. I didn't know it would be like this, but like this I had to know it would be.

Breaking off of work early, not showing up at all, working extra hard one day so the next day I can answer any questions over the phone, popping the little blue heaven.

I get bronchitis. I have never had bronchitis, but the flu and death are comparable. I am sick with that and sick with things and sick with suicidal sensibility. I am so sick with being back at the beginning, not having been to a meeting with other people like me in over a year, saying that my ideas are more powerful. I am sick with the thoughts that I haven't kept in contact with anyone I said I would, anyone I met in that righteous place, anyone that may help me stay sober.

I get a doctor's note. I get to stay home from work without feeling guilty. After all: I have bronchitis. While I am resting, I want to be wrestling, so I call my man and I get one week supply. One week's supply, that is all I want, and then I am done.

I start taking my anti-biotics and slowly over three days I feel better from the temporary sick, the permanent one worse.

Through a weekend I know the stop is coming, the end is near, the withdrawal foregone, this has gotten out of hand again. Again and again.

The withdrawal sets in differently than alcohol, body aches and sleeping. Just soreness and depression, sniveling and cold. Bring me soup and let me rest, and let me pretend to be the best.

Alcohol withdrawal is so so fast, gardening the brain, picking the weeds.

"There are two distinct classes of what are called thoughts: those that we produce in ourselves by reflection and the act of thinking, and those that bolt into the mind of their own accord."
–Thomas Paine

The latter is the alcohol withdrawal, the fast uncontrollable. The opiate withdrawal is a nightmare, but suffused with sleep and sweat and snot and sleep. Mixed with capricious mood swings and irritating irritability. And it lasts too long. I convince myself I need a little break, people can tell what is coming, I need a little break.

I need to feel different. And crack does that.

I go down to Colfax Avenue and spot my man, so easily out of the hundreds shuffling around. I can smell his Jaundice. An African man from Uganda with yellow eyes and carrying a backpack full of sadness.

It takes two seconds, "Yo, I'm lookin."

"Let me in."

He sells me two bags over the next two days. I get more pills and want it all to stop. Tomorrow I am supposed to go back to work, but I haven't felt that way for quite some time. I am tired of pretending, I am tired of putting everyone through this.

I take three 40 mg pills of quiet, smoke a twenty bag, drink a pint, and end up on the floor in my room. All is quiet and pathetic and foggy, not nearly as clearly as I can recreate it with simple eloquence. I lay on my back, sad from running out of crack, sad from still having other stuff. Sad from forcing my Mother and my Sister to watch all this with such worry at such close range. Their dear hearts have just tried to be encouraging, and stay out of my way. I lay flat on my back with my legs together and my arms straight out.

Christ on his carpet crucifix.

I am oh so, so so tired. There is a knife from work in my pocket. This life has worn on me, on my me, on my soul. The synaptic corruption is too much, and I just cannot feel better. It is a knife that used to be sharp. A knife that can have people in my life answering to people in their lives, "I know, it just more of the same." Leaving them with no one to talk to, everyone to my everyone has gotten sick of the stories too. I am tired of that.

This is not me existence.

My mom comes into the room and lies down in bed, I barely acknowledge. I see her shadow and here the bed squeak, but I am on the floor and I am worlds away, I am not thinking of her presence, not calling for help; I am not acknowledging the presence of the outside world either, just nodding and fiending and pulling out the knife.

I open it, extend the blade, and cut my left wrist as hard as my opiated body will permit. I cut my wrist three or four times, hoping upon hope that an artery will find the blade. Hoping to quiet the all. Hoping that this will really work, dazed and confused.

I cut the other wrist the same, blood spurting. Blood squirting to the floor. I cut as hard as I can, the knife is dull, too dull, but I think it has been done. I cut again as hard as I can, blurred vision, seeing red.

I lay back, bleeding. Wishing. I think it is happening. In my delusional, junkie mind, I think I am dying.

"Mom."

"Yeah bud."

"Give me a cigarette please."

"Sure." Rustling. "I have to turn on the light."

Pathetic little screams for help.

"I wouldn't do that."

"Wha-Oh my God."

She is dramatic and scared and calls for my sister, and for a second I really think I have hurt myself, and I smile. That gross, crying, helpless, smile.

My Sister lights me a cigarette and puts it in my mouth as I hear vaguely concealed whimpers from my Mother. I mean, we were in the same room, and I was using a knife that couldn't cut a scratch, but I pushed and cut as hard as I could.

The paramedics rush me and make fun of me in my treacherous incoherence. I end up with seven staples in my right wrist and five in my left. War wounds. No arterial damage, but deep enough to be just so close. I cannot believe all of this. It is sick.

I am sobering up at the hospital after refusing to answer any constabulary inquiries, after insulting the nurses, and one of the nurses says she needs a urine sample.

I don't answer.

She says we can do it the easy way, or we can do it the hard way and I tell her to go get it. She tells me it is going to hurt immensely but I don't care. After so long, I am finally aware that I don't feel so good, that I have been absent, and I want the pain. She tells the two police officers in the room to get ready to hold my arms, and the two nurses to hold my legs. She says get ready, she goes up. I don't even flinch, I don't even wince. My breathing doesn't even change. I am not totally drawn and drooling, and it hurts. It hurts. It hurts. But I want the pain. I need the pain. Everyone in the room looks at each other. They all walk away from me. In a while the nurse says that she has enough and takes it out. I tell her that now I have to urinate. She says she has never seen anyone urinate after that and leaves the room. I go fire, I go bad, this must be what birth feels like, and tears drop. She comes in after a minute and sees the bottle one-quarter full.

"Well that was impressive."

Am I really here for this? Can this be what my life has become?

After lying to the on-call psychiatrist, all about how it was the drugs and I have never thought of suicide and if I could just go home and seek the appropriate care, I tell him about all of my resources and background and education, he lets me go.

I get more pills the next day, so ashamed, so embarrassed, so halfway sober.

From memory to memory, there is nothing else but these.

The next day I feel so bad I start drinking again, pouring down pints.

Soon, neither my Mother nor Sister can resist it. We are one big happy ocean of loneliness, despair, and childhood crabbing. We drink for weeks. We wake up each day looking at each other to see who is going to say it first: I need more.

I am always first, and soon our room/house is an absolute mess. There is fighting and police and I can't believe no one goes to jail. I live each day over and over. Drinking until I pass out, staving withdrawal, looking for the keys to my car, not finding them, pawning stuff for more alcohol money, buying beer at the gas station on the gas card belonging to my company. Each day my only wish is for it to stop, but it seems never ending. The walls are at us all, we are distrustful of each other, always telling the other to leave. I am dirty, haven't showered in weeks, and the carpet is like the bottom of the universe. Earth on hell.

All three phones going off at different intervals, all hugging bottles.

I can't even muster up the intelligence or courage to hate myself for pulling them in. For starting all of this and for perpetuating it with the sun outside and security at my fingertips. For "attempting" suicide, for everything therein.

I feel like I shouldn't be here anymore, and the weeks feel like years.

I start calling people I know somewhere in the middle screaming and yelling, angry with chemical rage. I tell my Father that he is dead to me, after all he has done. I call his wife a whore, directly to her on the phone; I tell her that her own son hates her. I blame everyone and everything for not seeing me after I "tried" to kill myself.

I have accidentally lionized my life. I have always had a gift with people. Always, I believe, people have seen me with a sense of beauty. With a certain admiration, for my honesty and sincerity, my kind eyes. I am probably wrong, but I have believed. All of that is the same, but no one wants to come anywhere near me. I am the king, but with no pride.

I blame and yell and tell my Dad I will ruin his life, that he has been a horrible father. I tell his wife to go lay on her back, the gold-digging whore. Things only seen in the movies, things I can't believe.

I tell Mya I am going to kill her, I am going to kill her parents. I tell her these things for something that I am sure is mildly offensive to every other person not on absolute poisonous overload.

I tell them all I blame them for everything; for the drugs; for the drinking; for being built the way I am; for not trying to save me.

I tell them what I am unfamiliar with in regular life. The violent nastiness hiding in the back of me. In all of us. What we are all capable of with enough insanity. What we can be with our thoroughly tainted woes. When we are completely incomplete; perfectly imperfect. Indulging all our little ghosts.

The paramedics that took me to the hospital lost my driver's license. Days later there is an intake psychiatric appointment. The psychiatrist actually set something up for me. The night before I read up on it. I have to have a state ID or Driver's License. I can not go. I can get my job back, again, if I go, but I cannot. This is not doped-up, drugged-full thinking, I don't have a license. Instead of simply explaining to my Father that this is the case, he asks me why I won't be going, and I explode. Two days of yelling at everyone. Inside a spiral staircase of multi-level admonishments, I am drunk and high again and back and saying the most horrible things. The verbal Rape of Nanking. I am spinning around like a giant black hole, regardless of every stabilizing effort from anyone.

It lasts for weeks. All of us. Waking and being strangers. I have lost everything again. I have done it again. I have done this again. No more job. No more help.

Each opportunity for a break, I do not take it.

I have threatened Mya again.

I have threatened my Father again.

I have pulled and tugged down the two blood women in my life.

I need a little rest, just a little taste. I need this to stop. And I go get it. I have been taking the pills casually for two months, hurting with addiction for two weeks. I was trying to stay off the drink, but I have spoken of futility before. The pints are easy. Nothing is making any sense any more. There is no coherence, no more time.

The withdrawal is not easy. The physical withdrawal with the emotional attachment of the suicide and the yelling and the finality and the mirroring look on my Sister and Mother who don't ever get along soberly, it is awful. The pressure and the pain and the ringing of what I do to Mya. The run-on nature of it all.

I want to wax poetic about all of the physiological symptoms. I want to be Shakespeare and Twain and Hemingway, Jack London and Kerouac; I want to be Upton Sinclair and Ken Kesey, descriptive and informative and illusory and hard and sincere. I want to be Langston Hughes, T.S. Eliot, Emily Dickinson, Faulkner, James Joyce, Sylvia Plath, George Orwell, Ralph Waldo Emerson, JD Salinger, Franz Kafka, Poe. But I am none of these people.

I am just a junkie; a druggie; a drunk.

I am just withdrawing and crying and sobbing. I am just lying here on the floor, twisting back and forth. I try not to focus on what I have done and where I have been. I am turning the TV on for comfort and turning it off because of disturbance. I haven't eaten a real meal in weeks. I am swollen and beaten. I haven't slept in three nights and know that I have at least seven more days of days like this.

The sun comes up and I cry because I know that there are people out there going to work and living their lives and I am grabbing the legs of the coffee table, racking my head as I get up quick to run to the bathroom.

Out there people are going to the museum and seeing movies. I am not under the delusion that all people are all happy, but I can see them at dinners.

I am here swallowing Tylenol and Benadryl and Cough Syrup trying to come off of stuff that should have killed me aside from my sickly attempt on my own life.

Out there people are watching football and trying to fix holes in their tires for the coming winters; I am here trying to focus, trying to say over and over that I deserve another chance. Even though I don't believe it. I am rocking so hard, shocked by the ring of a phone or the closing of a door. I am here trying so hard to believe I am a good man. Saying it over and over, every time. Every single time I hear that I am nothing, that I am too bad to deserve. Every time I cry because I can not stand what I have become…again:

I...am a good man. Tears. I...am a good man. Tears. I am a good man. Tears.

*   *   *

Everyone is always asking me for an explanation of the idea that we may just be the most unique, beautiful things in the universe. People who believe in my mind. No one really asks, but for the purposes of my own internal dialogue, I will pretend it is coming from somewhere external. Because the thought of me meeting another being and just giving it things sounds very strange. Giving it some of myself, in any way I can. If I intellectualize the silliness of that, I can't understand why we do that. But then I recognize that in this case it does not matter what my head thinks. It matters what my heart and soul tell me. It matters what my cells tell me. I give these little things to people because, if I can make their day just a little bit better, then it will make me feel better. I will feel better because I picture them smiling and I too know what it is like to smile. And because our cells want to regenerate, they and I are attracted to each other multi-dimensionally to optimize the quality of our future.

That idea is the most beautiful thing I can think of. That is not an exaggeration; that is the most profoundly sublime idea in existence. If you can picture eggs in empty space, floating in the nothingness, capturing delicately the concepts in and of the universe, this is the most precious and marvelous of all. Intelligent beings that ignore their own intelligence to create happiness for other beings, that is why we are the most advanced, insignificant little big beings collected somewhere.

We start from a single cell, divide into billions, and when we mature, we get to think about and investigate why we may have done this. And then we get to form distinct relationships with other cells that have done this. And on top of that I get to really, *really,* enjoy doing this with others that I do not know yet, and be sincere, and have them pick up on that. And I am lucky to know the things I know - I complain a lot about the amount of pain it brings, but it also brings incredible nirvana and sublimity.

The addict in me can't even fathom being sober. The person in me can't even fathom Darfur. I can barely look beyond myself.

I know I have psychological problems beyond my reach. The beauty occurs to me sometimes, but mostly it has been the confusion and nonsense. I want to give to others and share actual time with them, but I don't and can't. I know have psychiatric cobwebs, sewn and grown into mountains of self-confusion. Self-delusion. I project the anger I have for myself onto the world and strike back when it reacts naturally. There is something inherently unnatural about that.

I have been believing in the dragging power of my addiction on my family, especially in ways on my Father.

Whenever I have come out of such a state, like the last one and the next one, my plan is to never go back and never accept money. My intellect tells me that I am not being enabled and I could spend days and weeks and energy explaining why I am not being empowered by the people around me to keep on keepin' on. Years of debate and dialogue explaining how my Father does bail me out, he does give me money after I have made a mess. But he does not enable me to maintain a lifestyle of using and self-destruction. He helps me, I do well for a time, and for a while things go somewhat smoothly and I work and show up and then I make one bad decision and make one gigantic mess of it all. And he helps me clean it up. Then I would admit that I have no idea if that is a logical proposition.

I am not driving his cars, living in his basement, accepting money, knowing full well that I will use it for using. I am just working at his company, driving his company vehicles, cashing paychecks from his company – it is not the same. I create a quality of life and then in a murderous rage against whatever deserves me at the time and once the chemical is in me, I break. I yell and use and then withdrawal.

Then he helps me pick up the pieces. I have been so concerned for him, so sad at having to know that everyone in his life tells him he is doing wrong, but I know he is doing right.

There is a difference. There is a distinction between enabling and helping, and that line has grown so thin that they may just be one and the same. I am not a loser.

There is not only in him a question of how many times do you help, but like stone in me, rocky and present, is there also a question of how many times do I accept this help without feeling as though my kindest motivations are being solvently eroded by my own impurities.

You see, my mistake was in thinking that salvation lies within. It does, but not solely. I have come to find out that the way to enlightenment is through the kindnesses and generosities, simple and almost unnoticed, that others offer to us, and us to them. The fundamental genius of our shared connections.

The way my Father refuses to let me go homeless again. His constant acknowledgment that I am good, but badly damaged.

I have another answer, again.

I have accepted the notions and connotations of peripheral people telling me and us that my addiction is only growing and we are feeding it. But I still will not fully subscribe to it.

After this incident I realize I have been wrong. I must admit to the world that my mind has been wrong, treacherous intelligence. I have wanted to prove the addicted community wrong, because of my nature, because of my distrust for anyone. My belief in my own soul.

Alcoholics Anonymous, I happily and regretfully say, is right. They save millions, and I can't save one. For me; against all of my fighting, I resign myself.

I need the chips; I need to pound my chest and announce proudly the number of days that I have been able to resist.

I have had a change of heart. I did not desire it, or go looking for it. After I tried honestly, so lazily and foggily, to kill myself, so ridiculously. I drank, more than ever. I went through the roar of a withdrawal the likes of which I couldn't have imagined. Every other pathetic withdrawal, no matter how bad I thought they were, paled in comparison. Loud constant cracking, and actually hearing all the molecules in my head bumping and shuffling together, like when your sitting on your porch listening to a beautiful hail. When I came out, something was very different.

I no longer consider myself a genius. I don't even think that I am all that bright. That was the alcohol too. I no longer believe my way is *the* way, or the only way, or how to get away. I have found that I honestly worry of everything, I never truly accept help, I never humbly say thank you, and not try to change the opinion of someone with whom I am engaged in discourse. It all happened, like I said it never could.

I haven't been doing anything that the AA community has taught me, I just didn't know. My way worked for a while, I absolutely didn't think I was wrong, I didn't truly trust or give effort to any of the ways I was told things could work. I was working and dry and am now jobless and wet. The pudding is in the proof. It has been a realization, a conversion, a complete giving over of myself to other ways, to say the least. I am saved now.

I will chase AA meetings, instead of chasing success. I will give of myself to others, other addicts, other people in general, instead of trying to take away their minor imperfections. In a world chuck full of hypocrisy and prejudice, I need to be truly humble, truly wise. Crack a smile at differing opinions, no matter how big.

I have been paying lip and pen service to these ideas, but now realize, have not been practicing.

I have to look at the fact that I am not the only one who personifies the me that is using, giving him a third-person identity with a completely different set of standards. Everyone in my life does the same. I am tired of being two people. I am tired of not enjoying the company of my beautiful little dog, that great furry friend. I notice him and his dumb little smile, are unconditional. And people do that too, in more complex ways.

I have accepted all of these things so briefly because I am smart, not stupid. Have I said that before? But I have not been grateful. Unaware, I trudged on in the front lines believing I was owed. I just did not recognize it.

I have been sliding on space, down to the earth, not being pulled by a Newtonian gravitational force.

I see the slide, and I am tired of euphoria. Over the smallest of incidents, the least exciting parts of a month, I am absolutely nostalgic. I feel a high rush, flying and free, over almost nothing, and then I come crashing down to the almost always negative.

Sometimes I see positive things, and I know that is because I feel positively. I know most of *my* life is subjective, feeling as though the complexities of my moods, flat or up, calm or ready, dictate absolutely the way I accept the world. This is not so for everyone, I don't believe, but sometimes it is frustrating, the comparatively mild mania that accompanies me in my way.

Sometimes this is not so. I am not sure what separates those whose funny little happenings are able to affect them in a way that results in feelings that are reactive, more pure in some way, spontaneously reflexive. With me, and I am working to be a better little boy, what is in my mind and in my heart is projected to the world before there is any external input. It is not fun living selfishly, shutting out the curious and sometimes awakening points of view of others. It sounds stupid, and powerfully inadequate.

Somewhere between neuroscience, psychology, psychiatry, evolution, religion, and the truth is what we are. The details can be theorized, but the experience can never be fully explained. Mine and his and hers are universally the same, but are individually, verifiably different. By the same I mean we feel fear and we desire happiness, most of us care deeply and worry incessantly about those that are literally a part of us, we exert energy constantly in the attempt to avoid suffering, and generally enjoy fun. And these things I can notice, I can acknowledge and interpret and recapitulate these days, and chase the sober life. Chase it and pound it and suck it and live it.

The me I don't know does this, then the me I love deals with it.

We still live in that apartment, but in three days my Sister and I go homeless. My Mother is now in a program. The house had us all at rock bottom. She is in a program for women who are finally ready to admit. And my sister is pregnant. We just found out, and I don't buy the notion that it isn't my responsibility. My idea of family goes deep, and when the other end of the line is filled with platitudes and advice on separating myself from her stressful condition, I can't fathom it. I will be an uncle, I take that very seriously. As cancer.

I have no job now, I can't go back to work for my Father, he probably doesn't want me to. I have made a fool of him enough times.

I have two days sober, with scars on my wrists. I have to come up with two-thousand dollars in three days, or, we live in the truck that my Father had bought from me, and then, after all the crying and degrading commentary on his life, was gracious enough to sign over to me. He gave me my truck for $1.00. He let me keep the company phone for now, because of his divine dedication.

So, I start over.

Mya and I are working, you know. Working towards something that feels like Box Brown. The slave who packed himself in a box, waited for days, sent himself to the North, and was opened up free. Can we just use a trick to become happy?

I am scared and frightened and closed up and boxed in, sending my body to places that may liberate it.

Mya is helping, in that magnanimous way she does.

She used to be the girl I would kill for when we first met. Then she became the girl I would die for. Now, she is the girl I want to live for.

But there is harm done and time needed and all that regular people require.

I want to write her story, write our story, but it is not mine to tell.

She is an angel, a Goddess, a virtuous and patient being, who may have had enough.

He who writes should not seek to say what may be said, but what has not been said that is yet true...

-Ralph Waldo Emerson

I think of that a lot, and wonder if I have said anything.

I cannot write about her anymore, she is too beautiful and true, and I feel I am only writing and talking to say what may be said.

I need more and more, more humility.

I see these poor poor people, with these sick sick souls, and I know that they are me.

I have been so lucky to have the people I have had around, otherwise I would have ended up soulless and homeless. And I have to believe I have contributed to people not ending up mindless. I have to believe that I am a good person.

I can count on one finger the times my Mother has asked me to use with her. I can count on no fingers the times others have asked. Sadly, I can not say the same about myself. But I have to believe that I deserve better, I deserve to be ok.

I am not asking any one, in any way, to believe every addict deserves kindness and understanding, trust me, some of the guys I have met in rehab and on the street honestly do not deserve it. But I am asking people to remember that there are addicts like me. Who, when sober, are truly, truly sorry for what they have done, and are truly decent people. I have to believe that. I have to remember that even dying soldiers cry out for their mothers.

I have to believe that when I was modeling in California, playing soccer in Europe, or falling asleep behind the wheel in an injurious fury, that it is all part of the same positive framework. I have to see.

So I close my eyes...I see me wrapped in a white towel, the movie's emphatic robe, sitting on a windowsill with just me and my Mya. Our children are in college and I am on break from lecturing on The Revolution, my new concept, and she has retired in her late forties. We sit and the sun goes down how it does so perfectly over water, I lean in and kiss her cheek and because she is who she is, she looks at me and we both know how lucky this is, how unique and special.

I keep them closed and see the lilted, withering hippies hanging on to heroin and free love, and see the gangstas in the ghetto getting guns and coke and gangrene. I see me as part of it all. I see I am a part of the whole, the middle-class and the world and us all. I have to believe the world exists without me in it, but it may not be as interesting.

For all of the reasons I end up needing to lie, for all of the physical pain, for all of the real depression, the real and lonely and suicidally intense feeling of loss without proper cause, for the potential created by substances toward the tendency of violence, the selling and/or complete disregarding of my health, my body, for the extremes, the obscene, and the forgetting and disgracing of the power of dreams, I still deserve to be me.

Positive self-affirmations and the corniest parts of the Christmas carousel.

I have to believe.

I have to believe in personal revolution, in Love, in and of itself, and the future.

I know not if I can make it, how it all ends, if I can take it, the depth of my sins. But I must still rage against the dying of the light.

I keep my eyes closed and wonder one last thing: Have I made my point? Being sick is insanity. There is nothing linear or predictable. It is endless, it is fractured, it is cyclical, it is unbearable, it is not living.

Life is impermanent. I am no fatalist, death isn't stalking me. I just needed to get this out. But if I *am* too weak, too addicted, and if I do not make it, cry not. For I will only carry to the grave with me the sorrow of an unfinished song. And if I do make it, I promise, I won't make any more promises…

THE END

www.ingramcontent.com/pod-product-compliance
Lightning Source LLC
Chambersburg PA
CBHW060750050426
42449CB00008B/1346